CW00547265

COBRA
Replicas

First published 1996
Copyright Blueprint Books Ltd

ISBN 1 899814 10 8

Published by **Blueprint Books Ltd., 1 Howard Road, Reigate, Surrey RH2 7JE. Telephone 01737 222030.**

Computer graphics/repro by Apec Graphics, Reigate
Page design by Ian Stent
Printed by Grapevine Print & Marketing Ltd.

Introduction

If ever there was an automotive shape to stir the soul, the steroidal lines of the '60s AC Cobra must lay a fairly strong claim to it. But with prices for the originals still in the coma-inducing league, it's little wonder that the kit car market has sought to supply thousands of enthusiasts with a means to achieve a dream.

This book takes a peek at all the current manufacturers of fake snakes, but rather than saying one is better than another it's been more a case of this is how one company has done it and that's how another has gone about it. When it comes down to the crunch no two cars are the same and, for many people, it's just a case of choosing the one that best suits your needs.

Cobra Replicas is for those owners, potential owners and happy dreamers out there who simply cannot take their eyes off one of the most emotive shapes in automotive history. Enjoy!

Acknowledgements

Thanks must go to all the companies mentioned in this book who let us jump in their demonstrators and thrash the living daylights out of them. Brave men one and all! Also thanks to the team at *Which Kit?* magazine for filling in some of the gaps and supplying some of the historical photographs. And to Ian Stent and Peter Filby for their written sections.

Contents

Page

Chapter 1   FANGS FOR THE MEMORY   5
Peter Filby on the replica Cobra scene

Chapter 2   HAWK 2.6   9
In the beginning...

Chapter 3   ROLLING THUNDER   14
Southern Roadcraft's memorable pair

Chapter 4   BRILL & TRIFF   19
Crendon's drainpipe-chassised 427 replica

Chapter 5   THE ULTIMATE CORTINA   24
Pilgrim's budget cheapy

Chapter 6   SILVER SCREENS AND SCRUMPY   29
How to make a Cobra screen

Chapter 7   THE DAX INSPECTOR   41
The daddy of them all...

Chapter 8   SNAKE TORQUE   46
A look at the Cobra Replica Club

Chapter 9   COBRETTI - THE INSIDE STORY   51
From the horse's mouth

Chapter 10   A PILGRIM'S PROGRESS   56
Father and son build a Sumo V8

Chapter 11   HEAVY METALINE   61
Howard Brooker's individualist approach

Chapter 12   AMERICAN CONTEMPORARY   66
Cheerful, but not cheap

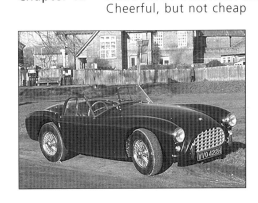

Page

Chapter 13   DOUBLE VISION   69
Two identical Classic Replicas Vipers

Chapter 14   KING COBRA   74
Sadly now defunct, the Unique Autocraft
Python was a notable car

Chapter 15   BEWARE FAST WOMEN   79
Racing the GD427 is girly stuff

Chapter 16   AK YAH   92
Spawned by the Cobra Replica Club, the AK
shows promise

Chapter 17   A WOLF IN SHEEP'S CLOTHING   97
Well, a Ram's clothing anyway

Chapter 18   SPOILT FOR CHOICE   102
Choosing from three rather different GD 427s

Chapter 19   DO YOU FEEL LUCKY, PUNK?   108
It's rude to point Magnums at people

Chapter 20   BACK TO BASICS   113
The slimline 289 BRA, under new owners

Appendix   WHERE TO FIND THEM   119
Names, ranks and serial numbers

Chapter 1

FANGS FOR THE MEMORY

Sorry about that title above but it seemed to be just ideal for this chapter! Peter Filby traces the Cobra replica breed's British origins, charting the births of today's market leaders and digging up every obscure marque he can think of.

WE DON'T KNOW WHAT CARROLL SHELBY THINKS about it, nor do any comments appear to have been recorded from the craftsmen at AC Cars of Thames Ditton who built the original chassis. It seems unlikely that owners of the relatively rare and rather valuable genuine machines are ecstatic about the situation, and it's certain that Ford, which owns the Cobra name, would prefer other companies didn't use it. But, whatever anybody thinks, one thing is solid as concrete: the Cobra replica phenomenon is with us for good .

Indeed, the fake snake's popularity explosion in recent years has been quite sensational. It must have been around the mid-1980's when the concept truly began to take off and sell in quantity, and today it seems probable that there are many more replicas than there are originals. So, regardless of the purists' disapproval, this remarkable modern-day reproduction of a classic 'sixties sports racer is giving pleasure to thousands.

To further encourage this line of thought, here's an interesting question:

could it even be that contemporary Cobra replicas are in many cases rather better cars than their forebears? True, it's a provocative suggestion that must inevitably create heated discussion, but there are undoubtedly areas of the copies which beg careful thought to give the argument ammunition.

Driver and passenger comfort, for instance. What about spaceframe chassis engineering and suspension geometry? Specialist car builders haven't been plying their trade for the last 25 years with total disregard for progress. Several of the companies described in *Cobra Replicas* have made concerted efforts to retain the spirit of the original machine but refine its structure, make its behaviour a little more dignified. And it's my guess that in doing so they've made significant advances over the raw material of the 1960s.

Today's Cobra enthusiast indeed has the world at his feet. For mega-bucks he can buy a pure original

This is what we're all getting so excited about. It's the real thing and worth a reasonable size fortune. If you want to drive a car like this, then the replica scene makes a lot of sense.

Above: This MGB powered BRA 289 was one of the first Cobra replicas to hit the road. Looks a bit bare without the more usual brightwork.
Below: Pete & Mart's 427 replica was one of the first big arched cars to hit the market.

and for slightly less he can talk to Autokraft of Weybridge who make the MkIV Cobra, a direct descendant of the original. But it's when he moves into the rather more affordable bracket of £8000 - £20,000 that things start to get interesting and dreams become reality. Not only that but there's suddenly a wide choice available.

Want a Cobra with a sophisticated chassis and Lotus Elan-style roadholding? You've got it. Fancy one with four-wheel drive? It's available. Tempted to stray from the original V8 approach with a refined Jaguar V12 engine or Ford's latest 2.9-litre fuel-injected V6? You have the option. Want to start at the pure budget end with a four-cylinder Cortina as donor vehicle? Why not? It might eventually lead on to a big money, 500bhp concours job.

Almost every conceivable strain of the Cobra breed is covered over the following pages. When you consider that the original cars almost had tunnel vision, today's replicas offer a vast choice of approaches. A remarkably healthy situation by Cobra standards. But where did it all start?

Well, the seeds for British Cobra replicas – and bear in mind that the original Cobras were based anyway on a British sports car, the AC Ace – seem to have been sown during the late 1970s. It could well be that John Berry and Peter Ibbotson, later to form BRA of Doncaster, were the first to actually get their hands dirty. Work began at John's garage/work shop beside his home in 1977. He'd managed to borrow an original 289 Cobra from John Atkins, a famous classic car racing driver. Trouble was, John and Peter didn't dare market their creation for fear of what AC Cars might say or do!

Based around an 1800cc MGB (later to acquire the option of Rover V8 power), the BRA 289 was eventually launched in 1981. But by that time the Doncaster company wasn't alone. Around 1979 time, DJ Sportscars of Ware, Herts, well known for its wide range of moulded GRP car panels and accessories, had made a Cobra body mould from some replica body panels imported into Britain by a German businessman. American Cobra forgers had been at work for some time before this, but this could well have been the first time a replica Cobra 427 body (with the bulging wheel arches) was made in the UK.

The German's idea was to take DJ's basic 427 bodyshell back to his homeland and use it to reclothe a Chevy Corvette. Trouble was, he only ever bought three sets of panels from DJ, leaving the company with the feeling that it might as well progress the whole scheme off its own back. Today, DJ's famous Dax Tojeiro is probably the best known Cobra replica of all. But more on that later. Back to 1979.

It was also in this year that a small hot rodding company based in Finchley, N. London, and known as Pete & Mart's, had started to mould its first 427-style bodyshell. Better still, the company sold a few shells to the UK market during 1979 and, not surprisingly, claimed that it was first to do so. The origins of the Pete & Mart's bodyshell are unclear (or, rather, no one is prepared to reveal the truth!), but what is certain is that the company also started work on its first chassis that same year. Sold off in incomplete form, this particular chassis – together with a basic GRP body – was eventually fitted with a rare Ford 302cu.in. Cleveland V8 (an engine only produced in Australia) and later returned to the company for final completion. By then Pete & Mart's had become Unique Autocraft, but the car still exists today and is almost certainly the first Python Roadster.

It was following a move to new premises in Harlow, Essex, early in 1980 that Unique Autocraft was born. The Python had indeed turned into a serious project by then, but the company's approach was to unerringly develop the car and get it right before marketing it fully. So it wasn't until mid-1983 that the first full body/chassis kits were sold.

Another name that appeared on the embryonic Cobra replica scene back in the late 1970's was that of Metaline, a small operation based in Ascot, Berkshire. Difference here was that Metaline's bodyshell was fabricated from aluminium. It was pretty damned good too, the boss being something of a perfectionist, and is still available today.

Meanwhile, back at DJ Sportscars other stirrings were beginning to take place. With the German businessman doing so little business, DJ boss Brian Johns decided to explore the potential of a Cobra replica bodyshell on the UK market – assisted by a new DJ employee. His name was Adrian Cocking (remember that one) and his idea was to advertise the company's basic shells (they had no doors or inner mouldings) in *Exchange & Mart*. It was around autumn 1981 when this started to happen and the loose proposal was that people should attempt to assemble these bodies around Reliant Scimitar, TVR or Triumph TR6 chassis. Some did – in fact, about 35 such DJ bodyshells were sold in all.

Clearly, though, these bare GRP mouldings weren't going to easily establish the DJ name as a brand leader for Cobra replicas. What was needed was a proper body/chassis kit. As luck would have it, the company was contacted by a chap named Dave Perry who proposed that he should design a

Above: DJ Sportscars was soon on the scene. This is one of the first Jaguar V12 powered machines. Below: This Brightwheel Viper came from the defunct Sheldonhurst operation.

production chassis for DJ and clothe it with a copy of an American made Arnzt Cobra body that he'd imported. Whilst Perry's chassis wasn't up to the job, his departure from the scene, leaving behind the Arnzt body, was quite fortuitous. DJ's project at last had a chance to get its act together.

Mid-way through 1983, the first serious DJ Cobra replica, now known as the Dax, was under construction. After a bare bodyshell had been displayed at the Stoneleigh kit car show in spring that year, all efforts were directed at acquiring a decent chassis that could handle small block V8 power and do the car justice. With both BRA and Unique Autocraft by now already signing up their first few customers, a new breed was seriously in the making.

A Brighton based company called Hansen Engines was the operation selected to design and fabricate the new Dax chassis. Resplendent in dark red, the prototype car made its full public debut at London's Motorfair in 1983, although it still wasn't a runner. The car's bodywork had been turned out of a new production mould made from the Arnzt body left at DJ's factory – now in Harlow, only a stone's throw from Unique Autocraft's premises!

One way or another, the Dax replica, still energetically inspired by Adrian Cocking, was rolling. Although a few kits were supplied in the latter part of 1983, 1984 was the first year of serious production. After that, it was success all the way. Today Dax is probably the best known marque amongst all Cobra replicas. A total of over 1000 examples supplied – for V8 and V12 power – speaks for itself.

Today there are over fourteen different manufacturers of Cobra replicas, all offering slightly different products. Exciting times for kit car builders.

Apart from seeing the Dax gathering pace, the year of 1984 was quite significant for another reason: Cobra replica projects began breeding with startling venom. Two brothers, Ian and Brian Nicholls, who'd worked with Hansen Engines on the Dax chassis, elected to make their own version, which materialised as the SR V8. Adrian Cocking left DJ Sportscars that April, persuaded famous racing car designer, Adrian Reynard, to produce for him a new Cobra chassis and finally had his prototype driveable on Christmas day. It was called the Ram and, predictably enough, took its bodywork from a Dax shell. In fact, this was slightly ironic as late that same year one of the first Ram bodies was itself ripped-off, given extra-wide front wheel arches and launched as the Sheldonhurst by a new company located in Birmingham.

The success stories of the Ram and SR V8 are well documented later on in this publication. But while these cars, along with the Dax, Python and BRA, were forging their reputations as premier division fake snakes, they were constantly having to fight off a wide variety of less talented cars that were competing for the spoils. Most of these arrived on the scene, stayed long enough to either be a nuisance or create a bad reputation and then either went bust or simply disappeared from sight.

Additional 1984 entries were the superb US made Contemporary Cobra (which was imported by a wealthy enthusiast based in the north of England, but only to the extent of about two cars) and the fairly awful AD 427 Cobra from a Colchester company called Automotive Design & Developments – it was run by none other than Dave Perry, who'd left the Arnzt body with DJ Sportscars!

Moving into 1985, trying to bite into the market

was Sheldonhurst with its Ford Granada V6 based car, Libra Cars of Wrexham with the Cortina based King Cobra, the apallingly badly finished Cheetah Cobra (again Cortina based) originating from Chester le Street, County Durham, and something called the Invicta from Invicta Cars of Hawkhurst, Kent. The latter seems to have been connected with the BRA 427 (which might explain why the Invicta name was never heard of again), and while the King Cobra found plenty of customers with its affordable approach, the dreadful Cheetah did its level best to spoil any decent image the kit industry might have acquired by this time. Mercifully, the marque didn't last too long.

By 1986/7, not only had Ford stopped everybody using the Cobra name but the list of options available to the d.i.y enthusiast had increased relentlessly. The Brightwheel Viper had been born out of the defunct Sheldonhurst (and had pinched the defunct Cheetah's name!), the excellent race-style Magnum had been launched and a company called Gravetti from Mere, Wiltshire, had emerged to maintain the seedy slot in the market vacated by Cheetah.

And so it went on, the Cobra replica scene shuffling and re-shuffling itself until it gradually stabilised into something resembling a range of high quality, properly engineered cars that did justice to Carroll Shelby's original concept. Today, all the second-rate snakes have thankfully been slotted into history, leaving us with a fine set of replicas of which Shelby and AC might just be a little proud.

True, they might not fully understand the virtues of the Cortina based cars produced by Pilgrim GRP and Classic Replicas (although these entry-level machines undoubtedly have their place with younger generations of enthusiasts), but they would surely applaud the finish and engineering of the current market leaders. In 1996 the advantage is that you can have your Cobra replica in a form to suit your taste exactly – anything from £6000's worth of easily maintained 'image' up to £20,000's worth of ferocious and engagingly temperamental, hell-raising thunder chariot. They never had it so good in the 1960s.

If you're considering building a Cobra, read through this publication and absorb its information. Consider the options carefully and choose the version that suits you best. Above all, always over-estimate on the cost of the project and the time you'll take to complete it. Having taken that advice into account, you're unlikely to regret taking the plunge. There are few motoring experiences to match the sheer exhilaration of driving a Cobra!

Chapter 2
THE SLIMLINE TONIC

Gerry Hawkridge has reached back

into the past and has replicated

the ancestor of all the Cobras:

and very nice it is too.

THE ORIGINAL AC ACE IS THE PRECURSOR OF ALL THE Cobras, although you won't hear Gerry Hawkridge use the word Ace in connection with this car at all. In his own version of replica morality, he feels entitled to copy anything that's been thrown away, but as AC are still actively using the Ace name for their current car, he refers to his replica only as the 1.8/2.6 car, at least until he's thought of another name for it.

The structure of the car is more or less the same as the Hawk 289, although the body is subtly but definitely different. Apart from the obvious bigger and rather prettier grille aperture area, the car has more of a "belly" than the 289. Gerry's theory on this goes

The Hawk 2.6 does a great job of emulating the earlier AC Ace. Gone are the big arches of the later cars and in comes a traditional roadster style with great beauty.

Above: Subtlety is the name of the game with the Hawk. Below: Triumph 2.5-litre straight six engine is the ideal modern choice for the Hawk and gives the car a healthy turn of speed and glorious smooth power.

back to the early days of Carroll Shelby's involvement with what became the 260 and then the 289 Cobra: if the wheel arches are flared, you can't see down the sills of the car clearly - so the expensive and labour intensive double curve down the bottom of the sill could be simplified and straightened out.

So when Gerry came to replicating the earlier car, his first move was just to do the nose, then trim the arches: at which point the sides of the car looked nearly right, but not quite. It was only on closer inspection that the curve became apparent: another few weeks with the body filler and the air sander and the plug looked spot on. The changes to the AC shell may well have been due to time pressure rather than a desire to save money, of course. The Ace had originally had a Bristol six-cylinder engine, but Bristol stopped making it. AC then turned to the rather good Ford Zephyr 2.6-litre six, with decent sized carbs and a bit of prep work by Ruddspeed, but AC customers didn't like the idea of a plebby Ford engine in what was after all an expensive hand built car.

When Shelby started shoehorning American Ford V8 engines in, rather than the British straight six, sales

began to pick up again, so the body change could have come about as a result of that.

In any case, the 1.8/2.6 gets well away from the Cobra personality, and takes advantage of the Hawkridge variety-is-the-spice-of-life approach to chassis design: you can put any engine you like in it, within reason. MGB 1800cc four, Rover or Ford small block V8, Triumph, Zephyr or BMW straight six, even an outboard Suzuki if you fancy it. However, the flavour of the original car really requires a straight six, so there are three options.

The Triumph 2.5 litre engine is a very practical option – with new crankshaft thrust washers every 100,000 miles it will run forever. It comes free with every scrap Triumph 2.5, and can frequently be found

with a four-speed plus overdrive box for £200 in a dead car. The Triumph's instruments are quite nice too. Less sensibly but absolutely accurately, you can still use the engine originally fitted to the Ace, the Zephyr/Zodiac straight six. These are rare, only have a four speed box (usually with a some remnants of a column change mechanism attached) and the exhaust manifold is probably the worst ever seen on a production car, offering a 30% increase in power as soon as you get rid of it.

Using the BMW engine is rather a nice idea. Bristol acquired lots of BMW design input as reparations after World War 11, and BMW then raided Britain and bought Rover fifty years later, so nicking a BMW engine and putting it in a replica in place of a Bristol engine does have a rather poetic circularity about it. However, there are lots of nasty plasticky widgets all over the BMW engine, and parts prices can be sillier than Shirley MacLaine. Of course, the long stroke 1800cc four that came out of your scrap MGB is not to be

sneezed at. No power to speak of, but lots of torque, nice noises, cheap to run and overdrive boxes are available.

The car pictured is fitted with a Triumph 2500cc six from a saloon, with a pair of SU carbs on it. These can be temperamental and have a tendency to dribble, just like children, but unlike children they can be dismantled, overhauled and made to work much better. Burlen fuel systems have bits for SU carbs going back to before 1930, so no probs there, and no silly prices either.

The 2500cc six used in the 2500 saloons and the TR6 is more or less the same as the Vitesse engine, so with a reasonably fruity exhaust system, you get a lovely range of noises out of it. There's a fair bit of power too, in a car that weighs about 17 cwt, although it's not the sort of thing you would want to use for any serious tear-arsing around. The MGB suspension and running gear is antiquated, just like the body design, so the two of them go together rather well.

The front suspension on the MGB is a sort of double wishbone affair, but the upper part of the wishbone is

Top: Same chassis is used for all Hawk models which closely replicates original twin-tube affair. Here you can see the MG lever arm front suspension being assembled. Above: Jaguar independent back end is a simple bolt-on option to MG live axle. Very clever indeed.

the lever arm shock absorber. These were all the rage in 1950, of course. It works well enough: the ride in the 1.8/2.6 is pretty good. On the firm side of comfortable, no funny business, more or less what you would expect from a good Fifties sports car. If you want to go faster, you can fit the Moss MGB coil-over shock front suspension conversion recommended by Hawk, which costs £400. Or you can buy a new pair of lever arm shocks for £16 each. The brakes can also be easily uprated with bolt-on parts, up to a Hawk-supplied set of vented discs with four-pot calipers. Mind you, at 17 cwt compared to the MGB's 24 cwt the performance of the original brakes is going to be much improved by the removal of several hundredweights' worth of rusting MGB carcass.

If you start getting bored with the MGB rear axle

instead, there are two options. First, you can fit a long Panhard rod, the brackets for which are already welded to the Hawk's chassis. This will keep the axle well in order, and will ensure that most of your rear end steering is intentional rather than the result of the axle doing a cross between the waltz and the pogo. If you've put a V8 in the car, or supercharged the six or something, there is another more radical option available across the whole Hawk range, which is to bin

Above: Hawk interior once again follows style of original car and is wonderfully understated. Straight lower edge to the dash is correct. Note the handbrake position. Below: Seats in the Hawk are specially made and thoroughly comfortable. Leather pockets behind seats are neat.

the MGB axle and fit a Jag back end instead.

Doesn't that involve a load of complicated engineering? Certainly it did, but Gerry's already done it for you. All you need to do is spanner up about six bolts and you can change the whole back end, even after you've finished the car. This is particularly good for keeping the registration number of the MGB, as you could theoretically register an MGB kit and then bin most of the MGB donor parts later. Not that one would condone such manipulation of official procedures, of course.

Mind you, the demo car, currently at CRA in Guildford, is just fine the way it is, built from MGB and Triumph. It's comfy with well cushioned black leather seats, the bodywork is very tasty and nicely finished in a mid metallic blue, and the lack of a scoop on the bonnet or a thunderstorm in the exhaust pipes makes a nice change. The doors are heavy with intrusion bars, and fit very well, shutting with a solid thud. The steering wheel is a custom Moto-lita, with a much smaller boss which allows you to see the instruments, a bit of a novelty for any car associated with a Cobra.

The cost is perhaps lower than you would expect, as you can choose cheap engines and take advantage of the cheap TR6 wire wheels at £75 each. Somewhere between £7000 and £10,000 should see you on the road with a decent car, a significant saving on the usual £10,000 to £15,000 for a respectable Cobra replica.

As to changing the pile of bits into a gleaming

projectile, this looks quicker and easier with the Hawk than with some others. The body is marked for drill holes, and the windscreen slots are already cut. The doors, boot and bonnet are already fitted to the car, and they look as if they more or less fit as they come. The panel gaps on an unstarted kit sitting in the workshop waiting to be sent off to Japan are better than some production cars, and they certainly put a Range Rover to shame.

Detail abounds. The wires for the number plate lamp are already glassed into the bootlid. When you open said bootlid, the hexagonal spare wheel well, exactly the same shape as the original and also made of GRP, lifts out for access to the rear axle. The floor of the car is a GRP sandwich with marine plywood in its centre. This is drilled every 2″ to make sure the GRP doesn't ever come unstuck from the wood. The shell is unstressed, and bolts down to the chassis down both sides, with various additional location points sandwiching the GRP shell to the chassis, such as the bumper irons, seat belts and so on.

The cockpit and footwells are rather bigger than the original car, which may well have something to do with the fact that Hawkridge himself is not wee. Still, good news for big blokes, and also for any bears that might be thinking about building cars instead of just hanging about in the woods.

When CRA build these cars, they like to take the body off, finish the chassis, then reassemble the whole thing. However, there's no real need to take the body off to build the car unless you want to. CRA recommend the car unreservedly, and are happily building yet another one for a customer.

The chassis is a twin drainpipe affair, with the main rails made of 3.5″ round tubing with 1/8″ walls, much like the original in concept but thankfully lacking the transverse single leaf spring suspension front and back. All brackets are fitted and the chassis is powder coated. Gerry Hawkridge's obsessional attention to detail and accuracy should preclude any problems with things fitting on, and in fact if you have any problems it's more likely to be down to MG than to Hawkridge.

I have briefly played with a genuine early Cobra, and although that had a 260CI Ford V8 fitted, and thus made correct as well as delicious noises, the car felt very like this replica. It had the same light feel and poise. I think if you rooted around and found a Zephyr engine, or even a rare Bristol six, and fitted the Hawk car with either of them, you would be getting pretty close to the spirit of quality British thoroughbred sports cars of the Fifties. Even with the Triumph six, it's not a million miles away from the feel of the real thing.

Hawk 2.6 really is pretty close to the real thing, not only in terms of looks but also in feel out on the road.

Chapter 3

ROLLING THUNDER

Southern Roadcraft used to build cars that were evil-tempered animals. Their tempers have improved, but you still don't take liberties with them.

now passed the torsional rigidity and crack test, the 100,000 kilometre simulated road test, the seat belt

Below: Two slightly different interpretations of the Southern Roadcraft theme. Silver car is ready for enviromentally friendly European markets while dark blue car is pure underaulterated muscle. Loads of fun.

IT WAS AN SRV8 THAT TAUGHT ME not to push my luck with seriously powerful cars a few years back. That particular demonstrator is long gone now, but it was the most evil Cobra replica I'd ever driven. The sidepipes were virtually straight through drainpipes with bugger-all silencing, the clutch was so evil you had to use your whole leg to move it, the camshaft was so lumpy that it would barely tick over, and the entire 400 horsepower came in with a huge bang at about 4500 revs. That was my undoing: I was going round a slight bend when the cam came on, and suddenly a violent slug of power hit the back of the car. A huge power slide left me on full opposite lock, on the ragged edge of a spin into a hedge.

So nowadays I treat Southern Roadcraft's cars with respect, although the days of evil monster SR demonstrators are in the past. The two cars pictured are relatively well tempered beasts. Not that they're wimpy or anything: they're still the pit bulls of the motoring world, but they don't have rabies any more.

The chassis has remained virtually unchanged for a decade, and has

anchorage test and everything else to allow them to be sold in Europe, although they can't have wind wings or eared wheel spinners or open cooling vents on the wings. I'm not clear as to exactly what danger these vents offer, but I think we should all keep well clear of them from now on.

Another of the sillier Euro regulations stipulates flush filler caps, and as the SRV8 is now sold across Europe, flush fillers are available from SR. Whether you want one is still your own decision in the UK, for the moment, but of course we must all be responsible in weighing up the risk of reversing into pedestrians at very high speed and injuring them with a protruding filler cap. Too risky, I should say.

The new Southern Roadcraft factory is impressive. I've been reviewing kit cars for a good few years now, and I don't regard big shiny premises on prestige estates as necessarily providing reassurance about the companies concerned: big factories mean big overheads, not a good thing in a patchy trade like kit cars, and I'm just as happy to see manufacturers working out of manky old sheds on a farm. After all, it's the customers who ultimately pay the rent, and you and I are the customers. However, Southern Roadcraft actually own their new factory, which is a different deal altogether.

They didn't get to that position just by selling Cobra replicas, however: "Roadcraft", as opposed to Southern Roadcraft, is a semi-separate company which imports American engines, and which is a dealer for Edelbrock performance gear. This has meant a completely different and additional customer base, and also means good deals for SRV8 builders as well as a reassuring level of specialist knowledge, particularly on Chevy and Edelbrock, the very combination I used on my own replica Cobra.

The silver left hand drive car was intercepted on its way down to its owner in Spain, and is a smooth and sophisticated vehicle. It's still basically the same car as the monster I played with a few years ago, but one of the delights of the kit car as a breed is that every single example is different. Boring old production cars just can't do this: even with the Ferrari Testarossa, if I took the number plates off, you couldn't tell which one was yours.

The silver car has an underfloor

exhaust system in stainless steel, and at town speeds there's just the hint of a rumble to remind you about the five litres of injected Ford V8 under the bonnet. Let the revs rise and the twin snarl from the tailpipes makes the point more firmly. The restrained red leather with the silver paint is upmarket and understated, and this approach to the car seems to have been translated into its behaviour as well as its look. However, as it's a customer car, I just gave it a gentle tootle round before returning to take the blue car out for a proper thrash. Sorry, road behaviour evaluation.

The blue SR has metallic paint a foot deep, a leery magnolia leather interior and big rorty sidepipes. This car follows what I regard as the best approach for kit car company demonstrators: the louder, faster and naughtier it is, the bigger the impression it makes.

Below: Big V8 mated to T5 gearbox is a softy compared to original demo car. Bottom: Interior has all the right bits and bobs but watch yourself on those side-mounted drainpipe exhausts.

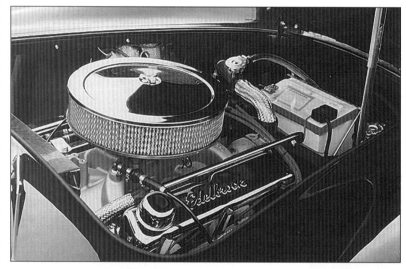

Restraint is all very well for Bristols (unless they belong to Pamela Anderson): kit cars are supposed to be balls out Fun.

The blue car is flash as well as flashy, a definite if subtle distinction. The huge chrome sidepipes are flashy, and the matching extremely-varnished Nardi steering wheel and gearknob are flash. Both contribute to the general persona of the car, which is not short of presence. Ian Nichols brings it out of the factory into the sunlight, and you can hear the 245/60 X 16 front tyres squeaking on the clean grey painted factory floor (flash, not flashy) as its nose emerges into the daylight and the glorious blue paint job glitters in the sun. (flash as well as flashy.)

"What sort of cam has this one got?" I ask, mindful of earlier experiences.

"Standard," says the other Nichols brother, Brian. "The old black demonstrator was a bit too naughty, really." That's reassuring, I reflect, and wedge myself into the cockpit. The seats seem more padded than they used to be, and everything is pretty well where you want it.

Different wheel choice is certainly striking. Side profile is quite different with underslung exhaust system. A real smoothie.

Turn the key and nothing happens at all. The security system is flashing a little red light, and you have to deal with it before getting any joy out of the ignition. This is a good anti-drunk system as well as an anti-thieving slag measure: it requires a steady hand to touch the contacts on the keyring to the sensor on the dash in order to disarm the security system. If you'd been at the tequila slammers you wouldn't have a hope of starting the car.

When it does start, you know all about it. The engine may be fairly standard, but it still sounds like an approaching thunderstorm as it gets going. It fires on a few cylinders, spits a bit and then explodes into a fearsome roar as you give it a squirt. Whether or not the noise level is strictly legal I'm not sure, but anyone who doesn't break into a big grin at the sound of a barely silenced V8 is probably a Volvo driver anyway, so the hell with them.

The clutch is dainty compared with the old black car, and the gearbox is a T5 five-speed, which means easy changes compared to the old top-loader Ford box, which was a bit like driving a truck with a dragging clutch. With the T5, you still have to be definite when you change gear, but you don't need Popeye forearms: the amount of power means there is still an agricultural element to the box, but I guess if you wanted a fairy

cycle you wouldn't be reading this, would you?

Out on to the road out of the Churchill industrial estate, which is fairly empty, and I let the revs rise to see where the cam comes in, but there's just loads of straight grunt, no funny business. Which means I can give it a bit of stick out into the country when I've got used to it. If you're going to have an woopsy, having one in a good class Cobra replica is a very smart move. However, although wanging an SRV8 though a hedge backwards at a hundred miles an hour probably wouldn't do it any significant damage, it would certainly have a less than beneficial effect on the paintwork, which would not go down well with the brothers Nichols after all the work they put into getting it to look this good.

The steering's quite light, in view of the fairly small steering wheel, and the car is easy to drive in town. When I went down to the Lancing factory, the Nichols brothers were busy busy busy, so there was no rush to get the car back and I could take it for a decent drive. The road from Lancing to Arundel skirts the Sussex downs, and provides quite a good variety of driving, through towns as well as open dual carriageway.

Going into the cathedral town of Arundel was rather a mistake, as the narrow streets are flanked by very high castle walls and ancient three storey shop buildings, and the amount of noise generated by the sidepipes reverberating in these canyons had everybody in the place turning to gawp at the SR as I grumbled past them keeping it as quiet as I could, which was not very.

Back out on the open road, and the dual carriageway with not much traffic allowed for a bit of playing about. At fiftyish, you can stomp the throttle either in third, fourth or fifth gear, and the only difference is the amount of noise coming from the exhausts. The kick in the back and the leap forwards is pretty well the same. A mere ton or so of car combined with buckets of horsepower means enough grunt to lose your licence in seconds in any of the five available gears.

The sheer size of the engine means that when you're cruising at sixty, the engine is barely turning over, and is virtually asleep, just ticking over to itself as you drift along the road. This is one of the major reasons why I'm so keen on big, unstressed engines: driving is stressed enough as it is, and anything that takes stress out of it is a bonus. A little screamy howly turbo engine is pestering you to speed up, come on, let's go, let's get

on with it, hurry hurry. A 351 cubic inch V8 is shaking its dreadlocks, saying chah, mahn, tek it easy, pop a can a Red Stripe and sit back inna sun. As far as I'm concerned, no contest.

On the way back to SR, I took the advice of the engine, cooled out and took it easy, leaving it to rumble and chumble away at 1500 revs or so. I popped Edward Van Halen on the rather tasty stereo and sat back as the automatic aerial buzzed and clicked up. A bit of fast and dirty fingerwork on a Fender is just the thing when you're bimbling along in the sun driving a Cobra feeling lazy. There's no grief from other drivers, as they're all rather awed by the presence of the thing, and you don't feel tempted to get into any racing in any case, as you have manifestly no need to prove anything at all.

You don't even need to change gear unless you want to, as the huge torque of the engine will pull from 10 MPH in fifth gear. You just drift along the road, knowing that even guys in forty-grand Mercs who can't take their eyes off the SR are wishing they were you. The triple bulge of the air intake and the two front wings rises in front of you and disappears into the distance, and a piece of open empty road tempts you, successfully, to change down two gears and plant it, just for the exhilaration of controlling the sheer grunt at your fingertips, and for the rising thundering bellow of the exhausts as the scenery blurs. This is good stuff, this is what we want.

However, before anyone starts sticking pins in little Iain dollies out of pure slavering jealousy, it may make you feel better to know that having rather regretfully given the SR back I went home in my own car - a shagged and smelly 1600 Cortina with holes in it. Oh well.

Now is actually a good time to build a Cobra replica, as most of the manufacturers have responded to the length and depth of the current economic depression by offering bargain prices. Southern Roadcraft have institutionalised this process by inventing a permanent discount card, offering money off various items which change through the year.

A top quality Cobra replica is never going to be cheap, but the quality of the kit and the reputation of the manufacturer is reflected in the final value of the car: if you ever had to sell an SRV8, you would at least be able to rely on getting a decent price for it.

Chapter 4

BRILL AND TRIFF

The place is Brill, the car is triff: it's the

CR427 from Crendon Replicas, and

Iain Ayre likes it.

THE CRENDON IS ONE OF THE ELITE BAND OF REPLICA Cobras to feature the massive four-inch twin drainpipes of the original AC Cobra, but the price is more representative of a good class Jag and US V8 replica. The car is as authentic as it can reasonably be, given that it uses Jag running gear: for instance, the engine is a Ford, a 351 Cleveland. John Kerr has a sneaking suspicion that the four-bolt Chevy 350 is a better engine, and certainly it seems to be better value

The outside may be similar, but underneath the Crendon offers the Cobra replica connoisseur something special.

for money, but the original Cobra had a Ford V8 so that's the end of the argument - the Crendon gets a Ford too.

The Cleveland engine may be a small-block, but that's all rather relative. It's like saying Arnold Schwartzenegger is small compared to an elephant. The 351 doesn't crowd out the engine bay the way it would in a lot of Cobra replicas, however, because the engine bay is the size of the Pan Am hangars at JFK airport. There was a surprising amount of room in the real Cobra's engine room to begin with: the 427 side-oiler V8 which was nicked from the aircraft-carrier sized Galaxie 500 sedan was not a wee thing, and Shelby managed to cram the 427 into the Cobra.

Below and bottom: Lots of attention to detail in the interior. Gearlever and handbrake look spot on. Crendon's own badge looks good.

For the 289 Cobra and the earlier cars, the chassis drainpipes were 3" in diameter, with 16" between them. When the seriously big engines arrived, the new 4" drainpipes had to be spaced 20" apart. If you measure up the chassis on the Crendon, those are the specifications you'll find. Even the crossrails and stiffening panels are correct. I recognised some of them from a badly crashed 260 Cobra which a friend of mine is recreating: although I didn't measure John's stiffening diaphragms, I would be prepared to bet that they're as accurate as they look.

The front suspension is also pretty authentic, apart from the use of Jag uprights and hubs. The fabricated upper and lower wishbones also retain the anti-dive geometry found on the Cobra, which was apparently the first suspension set-up designed on a computer. Mind you, the computer was probably the size of an Edwardian semi, and would in those days have been diesel powered. The castor and camber angles on the CR's rolling chassis are set up by shimming, and if you do the whole thing before the body goes on, it takes about five hours to get it absolutely spot on. John is quite happy to take over this and any other bits of the build, depending on which bits you fancy or otherwise: each customer gets their own bag of pick and mix according to abilities and dosh reserves.

The steel footwells are clad in stainless steel, which is neatly bent and folded to look very slick indeed, and the floor is 2mm steel sheet, supported on outriggers off the main beams, again just like the AC. The 2 1/4" underfloor exhaust pipes fit in neatly with all this to give quite good ground clearance, which is very important to John: his workshop can only be reached by crossing several really evil humps, one of which is so steep that Land Rovers have to use winches to get over it.

The back suspension features nice long trailing arms, which are a matter of some dispute amongst the Jag suspension user fraternity. Two major Cobra replicators say you don't need them at all, most keep them on for cosmetic reasons, and a few run into trouble with them. If your trailing arms are too short, the arc through which they swivel becomes quite acute, and as the suspension travels, it either jams, bends the wishbone or twists the chassis where the diff is mounted. None of these is desirable. However, in real terms, most Cobra replicas have suspension that's too

stiff to move much at all, so the problem is to some extent academic.

The Crendon rear end is in the same ballpark as the Southern Roadcraft design, in which the trailing arm is located on the same axis as the inner fulcrum shaft about which the wishbone swivels: in this way you have effectively a very steady lower wishbone mounted at three points, with no conflicting geometry at all. John Kerr's feeling is that his own trailing arms could be useful in stabilising any axle movement in extreme conditions, and in any case they're long enough not to cause any problems: they can't do any harm and they could do some good.

Mind you, on some recent production cars you can see the whole front bending if you hit the brakes on a rolling road, so worrying about the stiffness of any decent kit car chassis is pretty well academic anyway. On the subject of brakes, there is in the CR427 an access panel to the inboard rear brake assembly. Anybody who has been through the living nightmare of fixing these brakes on a car without an access panel in the cockpit, on hearing that, will almost certainly feel compelled to go up to John and give him a big wet sloppy kiss.

The rest of the Crendon's rear end is a matter of making the Jag components conform as closely as possible to the Cobra ideal. The Cobra had double wishbones, whereas the Jag has a single lower

wishbone and uses the driveshaft as its upper wishbone; but with the new arrangements seamlessly blended in, and with some discreet stiffening diaphragms drilled with the right size and shape of lightening holes, the general effect is convincing if not entirely authentic. Certainly the actual performance of the Jag independent rear end is not in question. While it is possible to obtain a more authentic rear axle, the

Above: Ford 351ci V8 gives the Crendon bucket loads of torque. Underslung exhaust makes this example less tiring to drive long distances thanks to more subdued noise. Below: There's always decent storage in a Cobra boot.

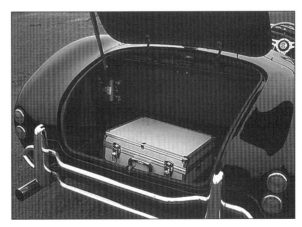

cost is massive and the practical benefits questionable.

The Jaguar axles lose 3" in width, because it was important to get the right size and offset of wheels on the car. While big offsets can make cars a little piggish to drive, with twitchy handling and the occasional kick back through the wheel, sufficient work with the kingpin inclination and general front geometry can civilise this, as in the Crendon. To tame the front end completely, John Kerr has also fitted quite a low ratio steering rack: the whole experience is lighter and less brutish than on some other cars.

On first making acquaintance of the very black and shiny demonstrator, the impression is that it could be a genuine Cobra. The wheels sit in the right place and have the right sort of offset, the dash has a flat line along its bottom edge - the legacy of a butch and basic sports racer design which very few replicators are able to resist improving. The instruments and even some of the switches are accurate replica gear. When you plop down into the convincingly and comfortably worn black leather bucket seat, however, there's a surprise in store: you can see behind you.

For a Cobra replica, this as delightful a surprise as if your favourite Kylie poster not only came to life and talked to you, but talked dirty as well. Convex mirrors mounted on each side of the screen, halfway up, give you a panoramic view of what's going on astern: most side mirrors on Cobras just tell you how fat the rear wings are.

Turn the ignition key, to be rewarded by a fat but muted stereo chumble from behind. The two underfloor exhausts are relatively civilised, although

Below: With its long legs and smooth ride, this Crendon would be ideal for the long blast down to the South of France.

you can't shut up a decent sized V8 completely. The 1992 five-odd litre Mustang that I hired on one of my more manic trips to the States was loaded with smog gear, catalysts and all kinds of complicated pipery and widgetry, but if you kept your foot squashed flat down on the throttle, it finally got the message and emitted a strangled but definite bellow as it lurched forwards. The noise from behind the Crendon gets a bit fruity as the revs rise, but it's hard work driving it fast, and not really in its character. It's certainly big and beefy, but it prefers to stroll rather than charge.

The gearbox is a top-loader four-speed, and you have to learn how to deal with it. Second and reverse are very close indeed, and the change is notchy and stiff. Not as bad as a Ferrari, but not the easiest either. The reverse lockout on the gearstick is merely decorative, but for newcomers to the car it would be better if it were a real lockout. Burble up to a roundabout, fourth to third, blip, and slot the lever into -reverse. Horrible screechy noises, bimble round for a bit looking for second, give up, back into third, off we go again. You could actually take off in top anyway with the sort of torque you get from an engine this size, but it's worth changing gear just to listen to the chords from the exhausts.

Right, fourth to third, double declutch, move the lever just a little to the left, tug back hard, back up with the clutch and give it some welly. That's a bit more like it. So you can either drive it firmly and decisively, or you can just bimble around in the higher gears - the car's not bothered either way.

The steering's very pleasant, light and easy, and plenty accurate enough for road use. For real high performance or racing use, a higher ratio and the resultant bigger arm muscles might be the thing, but then you don't usually have to do three point turns at

Brands, do you? Not unless you're up against Schumacher, anyway. The skinny rimmed Moto-Lita is right for the car and for the period: fat little leather numbers are really a leftover from Custom Car and rallying, definitely Seventies and not Sixties. In fact, as far as I know, a specific Moto-Lita design was original equipment for AC Cobras, although it wasn't actually the one on the CR. Never mind, it's nearly there.

The M40 is less dull when you're driving a Cobra replica, and a missed offramp gave me the opportunity to relax a bit and feel what it would be like to drive the Crendon over a long trip. Apart from the lack of roof, which is a matter of choice, the ride really is good enough to allow you to drive for quite long distances at high speeds. The exhaust note is always there, which is as it should be, but it doesn't make your ears ring when you turn the engine off, which most sidepipes do after a while.

Whoops, danger, Volvo alert. Estate in the middle lane, 55 mph. Prat. Why do they do that? Ignorance, or just selfishness? I think Volvo doors should have hand grenades in them, not safety bars. Their owners would drive a little differently then, wouldn't they? Overtake, keeping well clear. Off at the next junction, and a slick, positive gearchange, third, second, muffled roar and a slug of power shoves us forwards, third, top. A quick left-right and a hill, on a road I know well: I used to rent a slum around here when I was at college. £7 a week it cost, which was reflected in the facilities provided: it's amazing how much the human bladder will hold when the human in question has an outside lavatory. Still, the up-side was

Thoroughly convincing from almost any angle, you'd struggle to guess this was a replica - except for the fact that it was being used rather than cosseted in a heated and locked garage.

that the place never looked any worse after a good party.

Having got on to the subject of money, how does the CR427 shape up? Well, it's not cheap. Nor is it as expensive as it probably ought to be. The workmanship is impressive, and the commitment to giving customers a good deal is part of the price. There are only a few of these cars in existence so far, and they're pretty well hand-built. The aluminium inner body panels are fitted largely in the same way as the original Cobra, and look pretty similar to what I can remember of the dismantled 260.

There is always a temptation for a manufacturer not to dwell on the total cost of building a Cobra replica, particularly when his lunch money depends on selling the kit. There's also the temptation for a punter to avoid facing the real cost as well, in a sort of conspiracy to avoid reality. I know, I've done it myself. The fact that replica Halibrand wheels with tyres cost over £1000 a set is not something to warm the cockles of an enthusiast's heart, be he a seller or a buyer of dreams. Still, John Kerr doesn't bother with comforting waffle and bullshit: if you're going to build a CR427 it will cost you around £15,000 plus an engine and gearbox. Mind you, it will cost at least £15,000 to build any decent Jag-based V8 Cobra replica, and to get a close replica with a drainpipe chassis for this sort of money is rather good going.

Chapter 5

THE ULTIMATE CORTINA

Pilgrim's Den Tanner has a new

challenge for Cobra replica fanciers:

if you really want to save money,

you supply the labour and he'll

do the parts.

THE SUMO SEV IS THE LATEST IDEA FROM PILGRIM: sev means Special Economy Version. The idea is that you can get a Pilgrim on the road for £3000. We've seen some of this sort of application of mass manufacture techniques before, particularly with Robin Hood's S7. A complete car on the road for £1000 plus a dead Ford was at one time possible with the Robin Hood kit, mainly because of bulk purchasing keeping the price down. However, a complete Cobra for £3000 sounds pretty optimistic, given that you would expect to spend £10,000 on a basic Cobra and £15,000-£25,000 on a serious one. So how's it done?

The Pilgrim approach has been to cut out the labour element of the kit as far as possible, and to provide you with just the bits. For instance, the screen assembly on a Cobra takes several hours to put together, and there's a good chance of breaking the glass. So normally Den has to pay somebody to assemble screens, he has to pay rent for the space they work in, he has to pay National Insurance and extra tax for the privilege of employing them: he has to pay business rates, heating and electricity. Which is why even a budget Pilgrim windscreen is quite expensive when it's assembled.

However, if you just buy the bits and supply your own labour, work space, heating etc etc etc, there is a significant saving. Do be careful fitting the glass, though: all Cobra screens are very delicate and are just aching to crack. One injudicious push or pull in the wrong direction and pop goes the weasel.

The kit includes the chassis, engine mounts, gearbox crossmember, handbrake rollers, door handle plates, exhaust modification tubes, propshaft modification tube, steering column brackets, column extension tube, spacers and a petrol tank on the chassis side. The body and panels come in white only, with the door hinges but no boot or bonnet hinges. This limited gelcoat options idea is again duplicated by Robin Hood - you can only get a very limited range of colours on their wings and mudguards, because they don't want to get stuck with big piles of stock. Holding stocks of parts is expensive and we as customers are the ones who ultimately pay for it.

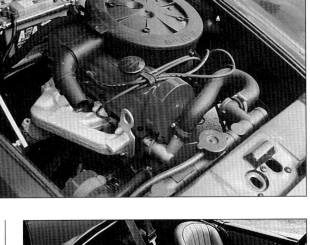

The internal trim materials are just that - pieces of wood, vinyl and carpet in sufficient quantities. Brightwork consists of overriders, petrol cap and base, and the pile of screen bits, including rubbers. The lighting equipment consists of four indicator lamps, two stop/tail lamps and a number plate lamp. Your headlights are still on the front of a Mini in the scrapyard.

That lot costs two grand plus VAT, which is not a lot. The labour element has been taken out as far as possible, so when you get the kit, you really have to get stuck in. The body is not finish trimmed, so you have to cut off and sand down other bits as well as all the flashlines left over from moulding. Metal components are supplied in bare metal, and the bumpers and so on require polishing. However, if you like working on bits of car and you're short of readies, it all sounds fair enough, doesn't it?

Ford provide you with a real bargain when it comes to the donor. I'm currently running a Cortina which cost £40, but it was only that expensive because it still had lots of tax and MOT left on it. The Cortina provides the large majority of other bits required to get on the road, viz. the following: engine, box, ancillaries, cables etc; rear axle complete; all four road springs; steering column components; pedal box assembly complete; brake servo and master cylinder; propshaft; exhaust system; radiator and hoses; wiring loom with instruments, switches, fuse box, relays; battery and leads; screen wash system; handbrake lever and cable; door trim rubbers; internal and external door handles and interior mirror; fuel tank sender unit; brake pipe unions; spacer tubes from rear shock absorbers.

That list doesn't leave much of the carcass behind, but you're still not quite there yet, as there's a small pile yet to be sourced from the local scrappy. You need to find a Mini for the wiper motor, wheelboxes and plug as well as a pair of headlamps. You will be less likely to

Top: OK, so it ain't a thumping great V8 and won't make nearly as convincing noises, but it's a start on the Cobra replica ladder. Above: Pilgrim may be the budget route to a fake snake, but the interior looks the part.

find two Hillman Imps and a Triumph Spitfire, from which you need bonnet hinges and shock absorbers respectively. No problem finding a Sierra to get the doorlocks and strikers and the bonnet safety catch, and then all you need is a set of 10" wipers and rear round reflectors. Shocks, wipers and so on are not worth messing about with secondhand unless you're trying to making a point.

New parts required are a set of wheels and odd fixings, nuts and bolts and so on. Pilgrim sell a set of wheels at £350 for four, which if nothing else are at least cheap. They're chromed eight spoke steels, and they proclaim to the world that you can't afford alloys. You don't need to use the usual very expensive Halibrand replicas to get reasonable looking wheels, however: I used a set of five spoke alloys from a Chevrolet Camaro on my Cobretti, and they looked the absolute business. Lots of spokey style alloy wheels will look good, but the eight spoke steels are really better

Above: At first glance who'd guess it wasn't a fire-breathing hellraiser? Just don't start it up while they're close by.

left on Japanese Barbie-Jeeps, where they blend stylistically with the white stilettos of the owner.

The classified ads at the back of *Which Kit?* may also yield a set of decent wheels and tyres secondhand, as many kits are made from Cortinas, and therefore by a logical process of deduction, many abandoned kits are also made from Cortinas.

So how realistic is the target of finishing a Cobra replica for £3000? According to the figures, it should indeed be possible to get an SEV on the road for that money. That would be in white gelcoat, with the Cortina components simply transferred without rebuilding anything, and with cheapo wheels unless you found a set of secondhand alloys for a good price. The chance of finding two Hillman Imps with external hinges in good condition is pretty remote, but Pilgrim can sell you a set of four for £35.60, or you can use your imagination and find some other way of hingeing the boot and bonnet: If you can build an SEV successfully out of the basic materials supplied, you can certainly figure out and fabricate a set of concealed hinges, which will look better anyway.

However, you will get a better car if you simply use the cheap Pilgrim offer to save money by providing your own labour, and don't try to cheapskate on parts. For £3000 it should be possible to put something on the road, but for £5000 you can build something that won't look like the cheapest replica there is. You can always get it on the road and then improve it as you go, of course. When you can afford a decent set of wheels, that'll help: when you can afford paint, that'll make a big difference too.

However, saving money on overhauling as you build the car is in some respects a bad idea. You can transfer the original axle bushes from the Cortina to the Sumo, but it will handle like a drunk hippo as you drive it to fail its first MOT, and then you'll have to change them anyway. On the other hand, replacing the bushes at £21 the set will transform the whole back end. Likewise anything else which is a bit dodgy. You can use secondhand Triumph shock absorbers if you can find some, but the only way to find out how much life is left in them is to fit them and drive the car. Buying new shocks in standard rather than adjustable form will not break the bank, although adjustables are rather expensive.

As far as donors go, there are thousands of Cortinas out there, selling for almost nothing. My own Eagle RV was built from a very nice 2300 V6 Ghia, which cost £120 and had an engine that at least made some half decent noises even if it wasn't as powerful as you might think, and my current winged chariot of fire is a 1600 Cortina which has a perfectly sound engine and box in it and cost the princely sum of £40.

So finding a cheap Cortina in excellent mechanical condition is no big deal, and you can just service the engine and box and bung them straight in the kit. The four cylinder engine does have a generic problem, though, although it's not a mechanical one. Anything that looks like a Cobra and sounds like a Cortina is naff, I'm afraid. It's as if Arnold Schwarzenegger turned out to have a lisp and a squeaky voice, or as if you spotted Sean Connery at Croydon station with an anorak and a little notebook.

If you fit a Cortina 2300 V6, you'll have to mess around with exhausts, and you'll have to take the jets out of the side of the carb and blow them clean every time one bank of cylinders goes fluffy, but at least it will sound nearly like an engine. Fit open sidepipes and a lumpy camshaft, and it will sound pretty convincing. But a small four-cylinder engine in a car that is supposed to have a seven-litre V8 in just doesn't cut it.

Budget for a bit more and make your SEV a six-cylinder with paint and some wheels, and then we're talking. The way to approach it mentally is to think as follows: a serious Cobra replica costs £10,000. So the original SEV price of £3000 means a saving of £7000. So if my budget goes up to £5000, I've still saved £5000. If you keep thinking that way, it'll make complete sense after a while, and you'll soon start wondering about running a V8, which is really the only proper way to go for a Cobra replica.

The Sumo pictured is very representative of the marque, as it's a customer built car that's on its way to Germany. Quite a few customer built cars have now been bought back by Pilgrim and shipped off to the Continent. Contact has been growing with Europe as the various tests have been passed: the seat belt and TUV bash-it-to-death tests have been passed for some time now, and the emissions tests have just been passed for certain Ford engines, so fully built low volume Pilgrims are on the way.

The blue Sumo has a two-litre Pinto engine in it, which is helped by having a twin exhaust fitted: it still sounds like a Cortina, but it sounds like a slightly fruitier Cortina. It does look quite convincing, however, and the wire baskets over the chromed five-spoke wheels look a lot better than the bare wheels themselves. The giveaway Pilgrim exterior door handles are optional, so scrub them if you want.

The car is eminently practical, as far as any Cobra replica can be called practical. The boot is surprisingly big, and some care has been taken to design it to be as big as possible within the confines of the Cobra shape. The cabin is well fitted out, with the exception

of two budget-related and very minor winges. The handbrake is too high and rather intrusive: but if you don't like the standard Cortina handbrake which comes free with the donor, you can always find a better way of doing it. At a cost. Also, the standard Cortina instruments are ingeniously adapted to fit into the dash with new chrome bezels, and they're set very deeply into the fascia, so the speedo's a little hard to read at a glance. Again, a set of nice Isspro instruments is an option - at a cost. (It's worth noting that the Ghia model Cortinas have a rev counter in the standard binnacle.)

Taking the car for a spin, it reminded me of a Triumph Spitfire, which is no bad thing. The suspension and general feel is taut and light, the suspension's firm and the stance on the road is solid. There is little temptation to fool around, as this is not really a high performance car, but the odd roundabout taken with enthusiasm revealed a fairly tenacious grip and no

Below: Pilgrim trademark is the centrally positioned inertia reel seat beats. Bottom: Standard Pilgrim trim kit doesn't have quite the finish of the more upmarket manufacturers, but it's still quite convincing.

noticeable funny business with the suspension or the steering.

This would be a very good car for a woman to drive: all the controls are light and easy to use, and all its road characteristics are safe and sensible. Before anybody starts, I know some women like pushing their luck in monsters, and in fact there is a piece in this very publication on Heather McAlpine, who hurls 500 BHP monsters round the track for a living. My own planned XK replica driver for the 1996 season, Sarah Johnson, would like nothing better than to do exactly the same thing: Sarah is the sort of woman who bandages up her bleeding gearchange hand between races and cracks walnuts between her knees.

However, it's the more usual sort of woman I'm thinking about, who goes to work and goes shopping, and likes something pretty to cruise around in that's fun to drive. I think we have to accept that seven-litre engines, straight-through sidepipes, three-second 0-60 times, competition clutches, brutal suspension and power drifting at 100mph plus are generally male rather than female enthusiasms.

Spitfires are light, easy and fun to drive, and so's this Sumo. You could happily take it on a long trip, and even if you had to use quite a lot of old Cortina bits due to financial constraints, there is the comfort of knowing that if something breaks down you are only driving an old Cortina, so the parts are a) reasonably available, and b) not expensive. I have sat by the side of the road in remote Norfolk with clouds of superheated steam hissing from my own newly built six-litre Chevrolet engine, thinking longingly of the old Cortina engine in the Eagle jeep I'd just sold. (As it happened, I got away with cooking the engine: you wouldn't believe how tough a 350 Chevy is.)

Overall, then: a bit of a bargain, and a flexible way of getting started in the Cobra replica scene. You can add whatever you want or can afford in order to upgrade the car when you buy it, from coloured gelcoat to a leather interior, or you can get a basic car on the road and upgrade it later. Of course, you'll then hear somebody throbbing past in a Cobra replica with a serious V8 fitted, at which point the smart move is to give your wallet and chequebook to someone else to look after...

Chapter 6

SILVER SCREENS AND SCRUMPY

Dave Shrubsole, aka Autobrass, has been making windscreens for Cobras for as long as anyone else, but he doesn't get many visits from journalists as he lives right down in the depths of the West Country. Iain Ayre dons bush hat and native guide and roots him out.

AUTOBRASS IS PRETTY DAMN REMOTE: THE DIRECTIONS in my grubby old filofax took up all of Thursday's space and most of Friday's, and that was after they'd been abbreviated. The far end of nowhere or what? Nanook of the North, move over. I knew it would take a while to drive down there, but the tape deck

Above: The extruded brass rod is cut to size. Below: Dave Shrubsole begins to mill out the hood frame slot at the top of the screen frame.

had worked its way through Sibelius twice, the Sisters of Mercy, Tom Waits and the Meat Puppets before I'd even run out of motorway.

After the motorway petered out, the roads just kept getting narrower and narrower, and prettier and prettier. I could feel my soul slowing down in sympathy. When a bunch of cows ambled across the road, my immediate rich-with-complaint Londoner reaction - get those things the xxxx out of my way - evaporated as I realised that cows can't get out of the way very fast, unless they've been at the BSE, so I just switched off the engine. What's the rush, after all?

Over a tiny bridge and turn right at the Rising Sun, nestling at the bottom of a cliff face green with ancient vegetation, the afternoon sun glinting off a silvered stream. More tiny roadlets, narrower still, and you can feel the grass in the middle of the road scraping the crud off your sump as you drive along.

Finally up a corkscrew drive to a very nice welcome. Anyone arriving chez Shrubsole is first quizzed as to whether they would prefer tea, coffee, beer, scrumpy or something to eat. Tea and so on having been sorted out to everyone's satisfaction, we all craned our necks to watch the Shrubsole family's next door neighbour ambling

Above: The windscreen stanchion, before being cut and bent into the correct shape, is clamped into position. Below: The completed frame iis cleaned, polished and sent off for the chrome plating.

languidly across the sky in his biplane. I suppose monoplanes are a bit new-fangled and racy for Devon, really.

The entire Autobrass concern is contained within a workshop not a great deal bigger than a double garage, in the garden of the family house. Despite the ethnic-sounding Shrubsole surname, they actually originated from the Home Counties, and only escaped the rat-race some 8 years ago. They have not regretted it for a moment.

Originally, windscreen manufacture only occupied a small amount of the workshop, which was also used to store the general crap that can't be put in the house. You know the sort of thing - ancient Lancias, Moto Guzzis, general accumulated detritus. All now given the boot except the Guzzi, which is allowed back into the workshop at night.

Dave Shrubsole has been making windscreens for

a long time. Panther Cars made good use of his brassworking skills for a good few years, but then they had a spot of bother with the Official Receiver, and a lot of skilled people found themselves unexpectedly at a loose end. Dave's CV also includes a stint at Dennis, the fire engine people, and quite a time at Brian Angliss's Autokraft concern, where they made aluminium-bodied Cobra replicas bearing the legendary name of AC.

And guess who used to make the windscreens? Correct, our man Dave. That was fine for a while, but the call of the wild was getting stronger, and there did seem to be a pretty reliable demand for really well made Cobra screens, so after a lot of deliberation, the covered wagons were loaded up and Dave and Sue whipped them ole mules into action and headed West, leaving the residents of the South-East to revel in the glories of the M25.

The actual making of a replica Cobra windscreen is exactly the same as that of the genuine article throughout the Sixties. The raw material for the frame is lengths of extruded brass rod, which is stacked up in a corner. A short piece of extrusion is cut for the bottom part of the frame, and a longer one for the top and the two sides, which are made in one piece.

The first step is to take the cut pieces over to the milling machine, where the process starts with cutting the central slot for the hood frame locators on the header rails to slip into. Dave's milling machine is a relatively recent addition, and is still treated with considerable respect. It wasn't an insignificant investment, and there was much careful considering of options before it was bought. The engineers who had originally been sub-contracted to do the Autobrass milling had produced good work, but in the end Dave's desire to control personally every aspect of the process won out.

When the milling is complete, the brass rod is then heated with a blow torch, and is carefully bent around a steel jig, before being annealed to relieve any remaining stresses in the brass. The top and sides, although considerably longer than the bottom, are much easier. This is because the brass for the top and sides only has to be curved two ways - firstly around the shape of the screen corners, and then across the car to follow the general curve of the screen side to side.

The bottom, on the other had, has to follow the general curve, the main bulge of the bonnet and dash bulge, and then there are two upward curves at the outer bottom corners as the wings rise slightly, reversing the direction of the central curve.

It's crucial to get every frame precisely right, as the whole assembly is delicate due to the nature of its design. Too much pressure in the wrong place, and the glass will pop expensively and terminally. (Incidentally, don't be tempted to grab a Cobra screen frame when climbing out of the car, as the result is frequently expensive.)

Next step is to mitre the edges of the top and bottom of the frame so that they meet at precisely the right angle. Following that, the little brass right angles that connect the top and sides to the bottom are fixed in, and the holes drilled for their stainless steel screws.

The frame is at this stage nearly ready for chroming, and Dave now turns his attention to the legs or stanchions that go through the bodyshell and bolt to the frame behind the dash, which can be organised in various ways according to the particular brand of replica. The screens are all made to original AC Cobra spec, and the replica manufacturers make their own arrangements when designing their screen frame mountings. Dave supplies windscreens to a number of the familiar names in this very publication, but is just as happy to sell directly to individual customers.

When the framework and stanchions in raw brass are exactly right, the whole arrangement is dismantled again, and polished exhaustively until there are no visible imperfections anywhere on the frame. It is then sent off to be plated.

When the frame returns gleaming from the chromers, the junior members of the family, Hannah and Daley, are in charge of the next part of the production process. For each rubber strip cleaned to antiseptic perfection with methylated spirits, they receive 5p. No freeloaders in the Shrubsole family: but the pocket money, although earned by piecework, does have a generous inflation clause included in the deal. There's also an adolescence clause, which must be coming into effect about now.

The chrome plating of windscreens is not an aspect of manufacture with which Autobrass have any desire to get closely involved. The chemicals used are unpleasant industrial stuff, not at all suited to a cottage industry lifestyle. However, in the same way as getting a decent finish on a car's paint job, preparation is all-important. If the Cobra frames are delivered to the plating company squeaky clean and flawless, it's likely that the resulting chrome finish will also be spot on.

The frames are handled with enormous care when they come back from chrome plating. Even the bottoms of the stanchions, which will be hidden deep in the Cobra body, are kept free of scratches. Chrome plating is actually quite delicate: even a dusty finger can leave visible scratching. Handling the newly chromed screen frames becomes very tricky in the fitting of the glass, which is the next part of the process.

The cleaned rubber strip is fitted into the channel in the screen, and the glass is very carefully eased into it. This is a part of the process that calls for real skill, as there is a fair bit of physical pressure to be applied, and it has to be directed in exactly the right direction or the glass will pop. Toughened screens are a bit more robust, but laminated glass - as used in Cobra screens - consists of two thin glass layers glued together by plastic, and all it really wants to do in life is to go pop.

With the glass carefully squeezed into the top part

Below: Daley Shrubsole gets to grips with cleaning the rubber strip. Bottom: Once completed, the excess rubber is carefully trimmed away.

screwed together, the excess rubber is trimmed away and the screen is ready for a final polish and crating up for delivery. Despite the remoteness of the village, Dave's experience is that delivery times from Devon are no worse than from anywhere else, although "next-day delivery" has a general tendency to be written on vans rather than written in stone.

The universal nature of Cobra screens - the same screen will fit every Cobra whether styled after a 289 or a 427 - has meant that we can benefit to some extent from economies of scale, and an Autobrass screen still only costs £285 plus VAT, with glass wind deflectors at £40 plus VAT.

Autobrass can be found at *Silverdale, Barfield Close, Dolton, Winkleigh, North Devon.*

Above: Complete with sun visors and wind wings, the Autobrass screen may not be cheap but it's certainly a beautiful finishing touch to any Cobra replica.

of the frame and the bottom part slid home to enclose the glass and then the whole assembly

Fabulous Hawk 2.6 shows how the Cobra scene took off before the big engines and fat wheelarches came in. Great attention to detail everywhere you look.

Southern Roadcraft's SRV8 has a tradition of being a bit of a beast. Tuned Chevy 350ci V8s are usually to blame!

Right and below: Crendon 427 is as faithful to the original under the skin as it is on the surface.

Exclusive Crendon will always sell in small numbers but Pilgrim Sumo (below) has had volume sales success. This privately built example is immaculate.

This Pilgrim Sumo was chosen by its builders because of its affordability, which in turn allowed them to spend more on getting all the right brightwork. A policy that's clearly worked.

Above & opposite: DJ's Dax is the big daddy of them all. Interior of latest demonstrator is unquestionably different! Below: This Cobretti Viper has Ford based suspension with Rover V8 engine and 5-speed gearbox.

Cobretti Viper is easily distinguishable from other replicas by its huge front wheelarches. Bonnet stripe gives this one a particularly aggressive stance.

Chapter 7

THE DAX INSPECTOR

Iain Ayre inspected the Dax big-block demonstrator when it was new, and was mightily impressed. DJ have recently finished revamping the same car.

I WAS QUITE INTRIGUED AT TO JUST HOW THEY WERE going to improve the car, as in its original form it was one of the best rides I ever had: the others being a JZR and a dark-haired girl from Ruislip. What was particularly noticeable about the big-block Dax was that you could use full throttle on a smooth bend, and the back end just dug in grimly and refused to let go, the result being that you were rocketed forwards at an exhilarating speed, and it was only your bottle that decreed how long you dared leave your foot down.

Below: Humungus Ford 454ci V8 is mated to a T10 4-speed gearbox and goes like stink. Bottom: Not to everyone's taste, but semi-wood veneered dashboard is certainly striking. Standard of trim is faultless.

So after a preliminary rabbit and a catching up on all the goss - they're a friendly bunch at Dax - it was out to play with the demonstrator again, two years or so after I first drove it. My photo gear in its "steal-me" case (the technical photographic term for an aluminium camera case) was stashed in the capacious boot, and I was slightly disconcerted to see DJ's Gary packing foam rubber around it: Gary is a bit of a maniac driver at the best of times, and this careful packing of the steal-me case suggested he was planning a bit of automotive ultraviolence. Fair enough, I have no problem with that.

What's new with the Dax demo car, I wanted to know. Last time I looked at it, it was a Supertube chassis with a fairly standard Ford 454 CI big-block V8, and a T10 four-speed. (The T5 is the box you use for small-block 5.7 litre tiddlers.) Not a great deal has changed, apart from the entire character of the car. This is one of the nice things about kit cars - if you get bored with one after a while, a bit of creative fiddling and you can almost turn it into a new one.

The main change that's not immediately visible is a small adjustment to the anti-dive suspension geometry on the front: they had noticed that softening the front springs didn't have the expected effect, and eventually put it down to an anti-dive related jacking-up effect happening during hard cornering, which tended to stiffen the corner that was under load. Anti-dive geometry does of course mean a compensatory jacking up effect, as does anti-squat. However, a small adjustment got things spot on, with the handling now more or less neutral. Another small change, reducing the roll centres slightly, had added yet more stability.

The biggest visible new feature is the size of the wheels and tyres: these are now a whopping 17", with Yokohama tyres. At these massive sizes, the Yokohamas are a stonking £250 each, but at the more usual and sensible 15" size, their price is comparable with BF Goodrich, and Gary feels they stick to the road rather better, particularly in the wet.

The new blue paint job is very nice, but I thought the previous dark greeny-bluey-turqoiusey colour was absolutely gorgeous: just a personal preference. The pastel blue leather trim job is nicely executed as well, and features a walnut panel in the dash with matching fillets in the doors. Not terribly Cobra in approach, really, but after all, why not? The seats have changed too, and are now deeper and wider than before. This may reflect the effects of the current economic depression, as it suggests that only guys who are old enough to have middle-age sized bums can afford Cobra replicas these days. Still, a Dax is a very effective way of stopping your mind getting old, even if you can't do anything about the onset of sensible Comfort Fit jeans from Asda.

The Supertube Dax chassis option is taken up less and less by customers these days, as it now costs £2395 plus VAT as opposed to the current bargain £995 plus VAT for the ladder chassis. The round tube CDS2 backbone/spaceframe saves 40% on the weight and adds to the stiffness, but most of us would have to be on the racetrack to notice the difference: the "ordinary" chassis, in common with most Cobra replicas, is as strong as a lorry chassis anyway.

There have been something like 1700 or 1800 Dax Tojeiros built, and bearing in mind that they are very fast toys, there have been a few prangs along the way. DJ's Brian Johns is justifiably rather proud of the fact that to their knowledge, only one Dax chassis has ever had to be replaced: every other one has been repairable with a few new sections let in.

The rolling gear under the Dax has always been Jaguar, and still is. There's no cheaper and better source of an excellent and over-engineered suspension set that can take the hammering that a decent sized engine and an enthusiastic driver will give it.

The Dax has been around long enough to outlive some of its donor gear now, however - the Triumph Dolomite steering column has become rare. While they are still findable if you poke around a bit, the design of the car has recently been modified to use the Sierra steering column and switchgear, with the wiring loom modified to take a plug-in conversion so that you can use whichever column you prefer.

The steering itself is surprisingly light considering the monster weight of the big-block V8, combined with tyres the width of oil barrels. The engine is well back in the chassis, which helps a lot: I remember getting stuck up a narrow track in a Dax V12 once, and by the time I'd got turned round, my arms felt just the way Keith Richards looks. The 15" wooden Moto-Lita wheel is rather expensive, but well worth it both in terms of looks and leverage. Leather trimmed polo mint steering wheels are okay for

Above: Single roll-over bar is an option over more conventional double width version. Dax certainly has all the right curves with muscle to match.

motorways, but a big diameter wheel with a good grip is what you need when you're parking. Either that or date Fatima Whitbread and get *her* to park it for you.

Dax's demonstrators are used as continuous test beds, and this car's original braking system had no servo at all. I liked the feels of the brakes, which required a good stomp, but which also let you feel what was going on through the soles of your feet. However, Gary felt that when you gave the car a real hammering, your foot got very tired with the braking effort, so they started experimenting with different servos, to get the ideal balance between lightness and feel. They've got it sorted out now, but the demonstrator had the previous servo still fitted when I drove it, and it felt a bit weird. Press the brake, and a few moments later the full braking effect came on. Not a problem, just a little disconcerting at first. Still, they'll have changed it by now.

The seats are definitely more comfy, or I'm getting old and fat quicker than I thought. Wriggling into the belts prior to going for a thrash is always a buzz, even after doing this for a living for several years. Poke your feet about in the footwell, getting the feel of where the pedals are. A fly-off Jaguar handbrake to the right of you, the kind that folds down again so you can get in or out easily. Turn the key and the car shakes as the engine spins, then it catches, with a muffled roar from the sidepipes. The silencers on this car are quite effective, and these are probably the first set of sidepipes I've come across which you could reasonably use for long distance driving. They're not exactly quiet, but they don't exactly give you a migraine either.

The engine had done 100 miles or so when I last

drove this car, and now it's covered 9000 or so. The difference is considerable, and it blips freely now, whereas it used to feel quite stiff. Of course, 9000 miles for a big American V8 is still barely run in: if you look after one, you can expect to get 100,000 miles out of it before you even need to take the lid off it. One of the big points in their favour.

The box is surprisingly light and easy to use, particularly considering it's bigger than a lot of European truck gearboxes. that's partly down to the Hurst shifter, which has to be carefully set up with all the selector rods exactly parallel, but once sorted gives you a lovely change. As a newcomer to the car, I didn't fluff a single gearchange, even when I was charging about a bit.

Not that I gave it any real stick. There are 500 ft lbs of torque at the end of that crankshaft, and 405 BHP. You can come unstuck very quickly with that sort of power available at the tip of your tootsies, and although a good quality Cobra replica is an excellent car to crash in, I'd rather not crash in the first place.

Below: Monster 17" wheels look utterly outrageous and even the Yokohama tyres will set you back a cool £250 each. DJ makes all its own exhaust systems.

So I restrained myself to going medium quickly, enjoying the power and staying in third and fourth mostly. The gears are pretty well superfluous anyway. With that sort of power available, you can charge out of a bend at madman speeds in any gear, and it just makes a different noise from the sidepipes. Third is a good gear, as you get all the power you can use even from 30 MPH or so, and it saves a change down to second when you approach a bend.

Gary is delighted with the Yokohama tyres, and on the way back he showed me why. If you floor it in the lower gears on a dry road in a straight line, you don't get any tyre squealing histrionics, tailwagging and blue smoke. You just get gut-wrenching acceleration, with a microsecond's pause between gears as your head rolls forward, then thump into the next gear, another bellow from the pipes and away we go again.

The 0-60 time is about 4.8 seconds, which makes me feel rather sympathetic towards Jeremy Clarkson. He gets excited when he gets to play with anything that goes faster than about seven seconds to sixty. Whereas I can't remember the last time I tested anything *slower* than seven seconds to sixty. He earns loads more money than I do, of course. But then if they wanted me to write about Peugeot diesel shoppers, they'd have to pay me an awful lot of money too.

The grip from the huge Yokohamas on the Dax is awesome, but Gary wanted to show me how the car drifts controllably when they finally do let go. By this time my head is beginning to feel a bit loose in its socket, but he's right: if you go round a roundabout at an insane speed, then change down and smash your foot to the floor, the car does indeed break away. Smoothly, progressively, and completely under control. Good job my cameras are padded, or they'd be charging around the boot like Mexican jumping beans.

In ten years, it's not really too much of a surprise that Dax have got this car comprehensively sorted out. What's slightly surprising is that they can still find the odd thing to fiddle with on a car that has been the grandaddy of the replica Cobra scene for a decade. They're still keen, though: they're still enthusiasts. Which makes a big difference.

A Dax is more affordable now than it has been for ages, with prices of £995 plus VAT for the standard ladder chassis and £1295 for the body. They can do these prices without going bust because they

make their own bodies and chassis on the premises. However, they won't spin you any yarns about finishing a car for peanuts: you can't finish a serious Cobra replica without spending serious money. Although the low initial prices will certainly help you get started.

There is also the option of getting some help with the build -if there are some aspects of it you really don't fancy, just bring it back and get some assistance. Some people would rather get involved with gastro-enteritis than wiring, for example, which is fair enough. Although the excellent DJ build manual, written by journalist Peter Coxhead, should go some way to reassuring the mechanically timid. Dax may be the grandaddy of the replica Cobra family, but they haven't lost their touch.

Chapter 8

SNAKE TORQUE

Snake Torque is the title of the magazine produced by the Cobra Replica Club. The Cobra Replica Club is where all the snakes go for a rabbit.

Iain Ayre reports.

NOT ANYWHERE NEAR AS SNOTTY AS SOME CLUBS, the Cobra Replica Club is open to Cobra enthusiasts as well as those who have the money and determination actually to achieve ownership of a Cobra replica. The only crucial qualification for membership is enthusiasm.

The Cobra Replica Owners Club is always extremely well supported. This is the annual get together at Warwick Castle.

Above and left: An impressive sight by anyone's standards. All types of Cobra replica are welcome and you don't even have to own a car to become a member of the club. Enthusiasm is far more important.

The Club's story started in August 1986 at the National Component Car Show at Sandown Park, when Python owner Tony Alderton took the trouble to collect all the names of the Cobra replica owners who had turned up. The reptilian egg of the Cobra Replica Club proper was officially hatched in April 1987 and it flicked its little tongue in and out for a year or so, with *Snake Torque* photocopied late into the night and sent under a plain cover to a growing list of members.

These currently number around 500, and the local groups are beginning to set up monthly meetings in their areas. Meeting up with familiar faces at the summer shows is always good fun, and anyone with a good idea for a social event or outing will get an enthusiastic reception from the committee. Naturally, there are other benefits to membership as well as discussing a shared obsession over a beer.

Of interest mainly to replica builders or prospective builders, there is first-hand advice available from the sharp end. This information divides into two sorts.

Firstly, although magazine journalists try to be balanced, and to get some idea as to the buildability of

a particular kit by looking at it with a relatively experienced eye, there is no substitute for actually having built an example of the kit in question.

Membership of the Cobra Replica Club means you can ask for advice from someone who has built an example of the actual kit you're thinking about buying. Of course, there are all sorts of other aspects to consider in choosing a kit - you may be so struck with some aspect of a particular manufacturer's car that you're prepared to tackle the build even if you've talked to an owner and he's told you it was a living nightmare putting it together. At least you've got the information and you know where you stand.

Secondly, if you've already started building a Cobra, you may find yourself at the point where Widget A goes inside Wossname B, except that the bar that should locate Thing C is a baffling half-inch short of where it's supposed to be. If you have the names and addresses of several people who have already finished an example of the same car, logically they must have solved the same problem already. Let your finger do the walking.

One thing to bear in mind is that all Cobra replica manufacturers are small companies working within a cottage industry, so all Cobra replica kits are hand-made. With the best will in the world, hand-made cars

Above: The annual track day at Goodwood circuit is always popular and gives owners the chance to really try out all that horsepower. Below: Le Mans has become somewhat of a yearly pilgrimage for many owners.

are not all going to be spot-on accurate. The production tolerance standards of the kit companies are not usually as bad as some mass car manufacturers (just look at a Mini crabbing down the road, or the yawning panel gaps on a Range Rover, and you'll see what I mean) but pretty well every Cobra kit will require some input from the builder in making it go together.

The Club's bi-monthly magazine is good fun, with regular reviews of different manufacturers, events calendars and advice about various aspects of building Cobra replicas, as well as good places to go for the requisite bits. In a random dip into various issues of *Snake Torque*, you are likely to find such items as a report on the Topless Beaujolais Run, goodies for sale in the Noticeboard section, an interview with Carroll Shelby, threats of violence for late subscriptions, advice on tyres and the story of a Sumo build.

Membership at £15 a year seems like good value, and if you apply the Club discounts to buying your Cobra goodies as well, it begins to sound like a bit of a bargain.

In the last while, the Club has become more and more active, with membership currently at around 1000, and the last major Club weekend at Warwick Castle attracted a total of 142 Cobra replicas. At Le mans this year, the club managed to organise 35 cars, which all did a flypast down the

Below: Any excuse for a party is always welcome. Bottom: Area meets, such as this Midlands gathering, happen regularly throughout the summer months.

Above: Most areas of the country have a monthly meet at a local pub to hear the gossip. Below: The author's very own Cobretti makes a rare appearance at one of the many kit car shows.

Mulsanne straight. Does that sound like fun or what?

Catch them at Goodwood in August for a track day, or at the kit car action days at Castle Combe, or if you've got a Cobra replica nearly finished, join in the run to go over the Stelvio pass, following the route of the Alpine rally.

Membership secretary is *Carolyn Hobbs, 01403 255525*

Chapter 9

COBRETTI
THE INSIDE STORY

The Cobretti name and product is as tough as its Jaguar suspension, and is still going strong despite considerable ups and downs over the last few years.

ONE OF THE FIRST THINGS A NEW COMPANY HAS TO come up with is a decent name.

"Cobretti" sounded rather good.

"You can't call yourselves Cobretti," said Ford, "it sounds too much like Cobra, and we own the name Cobra."

Cobretti Viper is distinct from most replicas by its extra flaired front arches. You'll also find a few changes under the skin of this example.

"Bollocks," said Cobretti.

"Mumble," said Ford, and went away.

The Cobretti story started in 1987, at which point Bob and Martin Busbridge were doing quite nicely as builders of all sorts of Cobras, but mainly as agents for the now defunct Brightwheel operation.

According to Cobretti, when that all went wrong, the company accepted the rights to the Brightwheel design, and the name 'Viper', in lieu of the money they were owed. They and their existing customers with half-built cars then got together and helped each other out until everybody was on the road.

There had never been anything wrong with the Brightwheel car, which was available either in low-budget Cortina form, or with a Granada base, or built from Jaguars with American V8s. During the good times of the Eighties, life was sweet: a well finished Jaguar-based Cobretti with a decent American V8 would sell for £25,000.

The new Predator model came out, fitted with a small but effective supercharger in the vee of the 350 Chevrolet, and chucking out some mad amount of power. The Viper's distinctive bubble front arches covered an extra foot or so of track, and the very hefty chassis meant a good ride and a very low centre of

Above: You wouldn't notice it from here, but this Cobra replica runs Ford based suspension rather than the more usual Jaguar stuff.

gravity. Regular readers will know that I finished up building one, after road testing a beautifully finished Chevy-powered Viper V8.

The reason for my choice was in the details, really: all the good class UK Cobra replicas have a lot going for them, and making a choice is quite hard. What I wanted was a car to use for charging up and down the country for 20,000 miles a year, so the cruising ability was uppermost. Also, the car is visibly a development of the Cobra idea, rather than an exact replica, and I preferred that approach. The extra foot of track makes a noticeable difference to the handling, too, as you can imagine.

The Jaguar rear end on the Viper V8 is used unshortened, and the front end geometry as well is pretty much what Jaguar intended. The Cobretti chassis is probably overweight by a couple of hundred pounds: even the plate over the transmission tunnel is 3mm thick. This Forth Road Bridge approach to chassis building means that if you hit a Land-Rover head-on, the Land-Rover comes off very badly indeed, and the

Above: It may look mean, but this Cobretti is easy to drive thanks to its light controls. Below right: Engine is a standard Rover 3.5-litre V8.

Cobretti chassis is still usable afterwards. See *Car Builder*, Jan '91.

The 300 BHP easily available from a fairly stock 5.7 litre Chevy engine will haul this weight around no bother, however, and although a sensible cruising MPG requires a very delicate right foot, the economics work out quite well in running costs. Rebuilding a Chevy engine is laughably cheap, and they're so unstressed and tough you can expect to get 100,000 miles out of them before you even have to take the lid off.

The Jag and Chevy combination is all very well when times are good, but the approaching depression, compounded by a government panicked into a series of expensive mistakes, burst the bubble. A serious Cobra was now worth not a great deal, irrespective of its pedigree and cost. The big Cobretti factory in SW London was still full, but it was full of half-completed cars that nobody could afford to finish.

With no end in sight to the gloom, brother Martin had had enough, and wanted to get on with something new. The partnership was dissolved, and he shot off to get on with a bit of travelling. Bob

Busbridge carried on, but the end of the partnership was translated by the gossip as the end of the business, and that stopped the orders dead, which then actually did finish off the business. The biggest losers were the taxman and the factory landlord, however.

After a rough few months, Bob collected himself together. There was no reason why he couldn't still buy bodies from his original supplier, and he had been working with Ferrari man Colin Bruce on a completely new lightweight Cobretti chassis, which looked very promising. Bob retreated to the long, narrow garage at the bottom of his garden and got back to work:

Above: Despite this car's cheaper price tag, it certainly has all the right bits when you settle into the driving seat.

with a good product, low overheads and a small but improving number of customers, things now look a lot better than they have for a while.

The light purple car with the white stripe is the first example of the new generation Cobretti Vipers, and it is designed to make the best of the available options. The new chassis runs a standard Rover V8 with lightweight Ford suspension. The componentry is carefully balanced: the standard Cortina running gear has been proven well able to handle the 200 or so BHP from a fairly standard Rover engine, which is after all made of light alloy. If a naughty Rover is used, the Sierra rear end can be used, giving fully independent suspension and a diff that will handle a fair old kicking.

The frequent use of the Cortina front uprights in all sorts of racing cars means you can get any of a number of fancy brake calipers, so budget Ford components can be blended quite successfully with the small V8. A Chevy would be too much, however: too heavy and too torquey. You'd still need the big chassis and the Jag running gear for that.

So, how does this new car go? Well, it went up against the big boys at *Kit Car*'s jumbo Cobra test day, and it came out rather well, considering it cost about £5000 less than most of the other cars there, and about £15,000 less than the very tasty ones. I drove it up there, just for fun, and I enjoyed it.

The new Cobretti Viper is a sports car, not a monster. There's a lot to be said for monsters, but not many people can afford to build them these days. The car looks exactly the same as the monsters, and it does have the crucial V8 engine to give it that roughness and the bellowing chords from the twin sidepipes that for me are compulsory for Cobra replicas.

The customer car pictured has only skimped on the Jaguar componentry. The rest of the traditional Cobra goodies are all very much in evidence: leather interior, lashings of chrome everywhere, replica Halibrands with spinners, leery sidepipes. Even when you clamber in, the illusion that you're in a serious top class replica is maintained. Press the starter, grumble grumble woomph. It sounds like a very serious car, too. As soon as you touch the controls, however, you can feel that it's a different animal.

The steering is very light, particularly with the big skinny-rimmed Moto-Lita as fitted to the original AC Cobras. If you wanted to use a weeny fat little polo-mint affair, which I don't, it would still be possible to park the car without enlisting the aid of Popeye and a can of spinach. The rest of the controls are all remarkably light too: clutch, gears, brakes. The contrast is similar to the difference between an MGB and an MG Midget, or if you like between an Austin A60 and a Morris Minor, which is what the MGs are under the skin.

Jag and Chevy Cobras have notchy gear changes, stomp brakes and meaty clutches: you know that you're dealing with big boys' toys. This new Cobretti, in contrast, is a lightweight sports car, probably more in the mould of the predecessors of the 427 such as the Ace.

The very wide front track means the same go-kart stability you feel in the bigger Cobrettis, and the added advantage of that set-up is that the wheels don't need massive offsets. This means that the steering weight and geometry is pretty well standard Ford, which in turn means it won't try to take your thumbs off if you hit a bump on lock.

The Rover V8 in a fairly light car gives a respectable amount of power, and makes the full range of all the right noises as you blip and flick up and down the box. This is not a demanding or challenging car by any means, and it has no massive reserves of grunt just waiting to slam you into the back of the seat as the cam smacks into song: but it's fun, it's nice to drive, it looks the business and it's £5000 cheaper than the big boys.

Chapter 10

A PILGRIM'S PROGRESS

This Granada-based Pilgrim V8 was something of a family affair, built by Darren Jones and his father Bob: and a very nice job they made of it too.

I FIRST SAW THIS CAR AT THE STONELEIGH SHOW where it sat gleaming on the *Which Kit?* stand. I thought it looked pretty tasty, and it didn't even cross

my mind that it was a budget Cobra replica: the added door-handles would normally have been a Pilgrim giveaway, but this one doesn't have them fitted.

The car is the result of a whole lot of hard and careful work, and looks the absolute business: as the Romans would have put it, *in veritas testiculae canis*. The first question was why people who were in search of an automotive Holy Grail started with a low budget replica instead of heading off to the loftier end of the market?

The word "budget" was the key. For about £15,000 you can either afford a fairly basic Jag and Chevy Cobra replica, or you can have a Pilgrim with all the bells and whistles. As ultimate performance, muscle and handling were of less importance to Darren and Bob, they decided to go the budget route. This makes complete sense, of course: for the extra thousands spent on rebuilding Jaguar suspension and fuelling a 5.7 litre engine, the difference in ordinary use is minimal. The Rover hasn't got the bass exhaust note or the torque and punch of a really big engine, and the weight and design of the Jaguar running gear gives you superb ride and handling, but most of the time it makes little practical difference what's under the fibreglass.

The project started in the wet summer of 1993. The family were sat in a damp caravan, gazing out of the window at their summer holiday weather rumbling across leaden skies and trickling down the windows, so they went and got a copy of *Which Kit?*. The idea of building a Cobra replica growed and growed, and soon a sheaf of brochures was spread out on the floor.

A few factory visits, and the Pilgrim was chosen. A visit to Beaulieu secured some pictures of a real 427, and the next thirteen months were to be spent trying to make the Pilgrim look as close as possible to the genuine article. As with all but the top kits, a fair bit of work went into making everything fit just so. It's relatively easy to make things go together adequately, but making them go together exactly right takes a bit of time and dedication.

The mechanicals in the Granada-based Pilgrim are fairly straightforward. The rear end is a strong, independently suspended axle which will take the power from a Rover, no bother. A quick and reasonably cheap overhaul saw it in top nick and fitted to the chassis. The front end is Cortina: when wondering whether the Cortina stuff is up to the task of handling a Rover V8, it helps to know that a hell of a lot of racing cars use the very same Cortina uprights to great effect. Considering the wheel-bending abuse given their cars by some Club drivers on the circuit, I think we can take it that the Cortina uprights will do nicely.

The engine on the Jones' Pilgrim was a 90,000 mile number that still ran okay. By the time they'd finished with it, you could eat your dinner off it, although you couldn't cook your dinner on it, because a Sierra Diesel radiator and two Cosworth fans keep it cool. It will need those fans, however, as it's now bored out to 3.9 litres, and once it's run in, it will be given some enthusiastic use. At the moment, it's only done 600 miles or so and is being treated with respect.

The basic shell has had little additional work, other than being fitted very carefully, with bob-weights, spirit levels and so on. Incidentally, I heard about a new apprentice wind-up the other day, along the lines of "go and ask the storeman for a long wait and a left-handed screwdriver" and so on: Rob Budd at Eagle sent his apprentice off to get a new bubble for the spirit level, as the old one was too slow.

The inner wings and arches on the Pilgrim were rethought to some extent, partly because the body is a new-style one with a deeper rear valance, but the boot mouldings weren't. Having got used to the idea that the inner mouldings could be used as suggestions rather than as gospel, they cheerfully started chopping up anything else that didn't quite fit. Nothing alarming, just things like the GRP seat pans being interfered with by the suspension mounts. The underbonnet are also came in for some serious attention, as you can see from the photos: there was no problem with the standard stuff, it was just that it was low budget fibreglass, and they wanted lots of shiny metal instead.

This makes lots of sense: the Pilgrim underbonnet GRP comes free with the kit, but ally and stainless sheeting is not frighteningly expensive, so throwing the GRP away is no big deal. The cost of pre-cut stainless steel engine bay dress-up kits from some of

Below: Latest Pilgrim bodies have more detailing around both front and rear wheelarches. Telltale Pilgrim door handles have been removed on this example and ride height looks spot on.

the tastier replicas is another matter, and in some cases would be enough to send Donald Trump into a gibbering frenzy. Darren and Bob's metal-only policy under the bonnet has been taken to extremes: even the washer bottle is made from an aluminium water bottle bought from a mountain shop. Or to be more accurate, a mountaineering shop. The only plakky bits left are the transparent brake fluid reservoir and the battery isolator key.

The Joneses were both lucky and unlucky in having one Norman Hitchman for a neighbour. Norman is 76 years old and an ex-aircraft engineer, and made a significant contribution to the engine bay area in particular. The lucky bit about having Norman around was that he fabricated a lot of the fancy parts under the bonnet with absolute precision, and he also used fibre washers on every rivet to isolate the aluminium from the steel, in order to avoid any electrolytic corrosion. The unlucky side of having Norman around was that if either Darren or Bob got something a thousandth of an inch out of place, Norman would give them a seriously hard time until they got it up to his standards.

On the road, the car is very impressive. It's smooth and quiet, and feels very solid indeed, with no rattles at all. Part of this is down to some extra woodwork which has been introduced. This is a good idea that could be applied to a lot of cars. What the Joneses did was to make thin plywood bulkheads to go inside the bodywork in various places, for instance along the sills and inside the front wings: these areas were then filled with expanding foam. This increases strength and rigidity, helps a lot with crash protection, and also acts as a very effective noise insulator. A smart move. I did foam-fill the sills on my own Cobra, and also the roll over bar, but I didn't think of bulkheads.

Another smart move was to use body filler wherever a double skinned panel had to be drilled through, for instance where the bonnet clamp handles go through the bonnet: the whole space was stuffed with filler before drilling, which makes the whole area rock solid.

When the bodywork and engine bay were being rethought, the future removal of the engine and box along with all the other major components was carefully considered. This was just as well in view of the gearbox problems that arose. Nothing serious, just that second gear was a bit of a pig to get into. The box was removed and "reconditioned", but the problem remained exactly the same.

The cause was apparently a synchro slip ring that becomes glazed, and requires shot peening before it

Top: Engine bay of this privately built example is immaculate and shows what can be achieved by the competent builder. Engine is 3.5-litre Rover that has been bored out to 3.9-litres. Above: Dash has been nicely finished. Note the retro gear lever.

will do its job again: if you have a Rover box that misbehaves in that way, it would be worth assuming that having it "reconditioned" without specifying slip ring shot peening will be about as much use as having your car "serviced" at a garage. (According to Which? magazine, 1 in 30 garages do a service adequately. Reconditioning seems to be a similar lottery)

The two Joneses can now get the gearbox out in 45 minutes, although with the problem now apparently sorted out, it should be able to stay in place for a while. Access to other areas has also been considered. There is a set of holes adjacent to the mountings for the bumpers, for instance, so that you can adjust their position in relation to the bodywork.

The interior is all Pilgrim, apart from the plates and gaiters for the handbrake and gear lever. The recommended Granada steering wheel cowl is rather square and looked a little odd in such a generally round and curvy car, so Bob and Darren rooted around in a scrapyard and found a Cortina one. With a bit of hacking and a grey trim job, it looks very nice. The

Above: Darren Jones, and his father Bob, have built an absolutely cracking Cobra replica by buying at the cheaper end of the market in order to afford all the right bits and pieces. The success of that policy is clear for everyone to see.

Moto-Lita wooden steering is the finishing touch for the cockpit: these look even better in the bigger 16" size, but they're still the correct wheel for the car, and incidentally a Moto-Lita wheel was original equipment on the AC Cobra.

The pedals are now alloy replica AC items, mounted higher up to get them more on the ball of the foot, and the floor mats are a bit tasty. They've had big rectangular patches burnt and shaved off, so that Cobra logos could be let into them. Trouble is, they look so nice they're kept in plastic bags to protect them. Which is a bit like wearing galoshes over your wellies.

The exhaust note from the sidepipes is quite pleasing: nicely bassy and fruity, and noisy enough to make the point, but not noisy enough to give you a headache, which can be a real problem with some of the bigger engines and naughtier pipes. The Joneses had a bit of a go at the silencing, and in the end removed one baffle. At the business end of the exhaust, the four primary pipes converge on a surprisingly small single pipe leading out of the engine bay: it would be worth changing that for something of a larger bore, as it can't be good for gas flow. It does get a bit crowded in there, and it doesn't look as though there would be room for a serious set of headers: but then it is only the small V8.

Are the Joneses happy with the car? Yes, well pleased with it. It took 13 months to build, which was pretty close to their estimate, and it cost £16,800 in total, which was also pretty well what they had budgeted for. They ran over budget in the end by £300, which is the most accurate build budget I have ever heard of: many finished projects finish up 100% over budget, as I know to my cost.

Some of the details could be of help to other builders, such as knowing that when Audi Coupe/Quattro bootlid gas rams are too knackered to hold the Audi bootlid up any more, they're just right for holding up Pilgrim bonnets. Also, a gas pipe T-piece fitted with a bleed valve and let into the top hose is an excellent place to bleed the water system, and a gas bleed valve will quite happily bleed water instead. They're not picky and they don't belong to a union, unless it's a pipe union...

Chapter 11

HEAVY METALINE

Packing a rebuilt 428 CI Ford V8 and some tasty detailing, Howard Brooker's Metaline 690 does the business.

Iain Ayre investigates.

HOWARD BROOKER HAS QUIETLY BEEN BUILDING replica Cobras for a decade or so, having got badly bored - and quite justifiably so - with designing credit card machines. Most of us haven't heard of him because he's always sold his cars by word of mouth rather than by advertising: as they're pretty expensive, he's never needed to sell a large volume of kits. If you buy a Brooker badged car, that means a fully built finished car with a Kevlar body: this is an expensive procedure, although not as expensive as buying a TVR.

If you buy a Metaline 690, that means you're buying a GRP bodied kit: still expensive, but you won't have to

Styled in the sixties, engineered for the nineties - hence the Metaline 690.

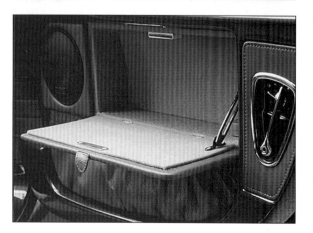

Left: Ford 428ci V8 is about as close as you can get to the original 427ci engine used in the originals. Below: Door detailing is typical of the level of finish to be found all over the Metaline.

sell your house. Why is it expensive? The first clue to that is visible inside the doors. With most Cobra replicas, you get a bit of trim inside the door, and if it's an upmarket kit, you get leather trimmed board with maybe a door pocket stitched on in ruched leather. With the Metaline, each door comes with a package that is more complex than the entire interior in some cars.

You get a speaker mounted in an acoustic box; then you get a lined storage area with a leather trimmed lid that folds down: then you get a door latch in a custom leather-trimmed panel that uses Spridget mechanisms to give you a proper door handle, rather than the usual MG latches: then you get the stretchy leather door pocket as well. The whole lot is fitted into shaped compartments in the inner door skin, which has been designed to suit, rather than adapted from a vaguely Cobra shaped door inner like most kits.

That gives you an idea of the obsessive attention to detail that has gone into this car. Another part of its flavour is the accuracy of the shell: looking at the critical area where the door top at the front fits against the bodywork, most Cobra replica makers have accepted that the body is GRP and this area is normally made quite thick. The few cars that have been moulded directly from an aluminium body have very thin GRP in this area, just like the ally body. The Contemporary is another car that looks good in this area.

The secret of this accuracy is that the body from which the Metaline was moulded is quite possibly an original AC 427 body that was never fitted to a car. The story is that the wildest arches appeared on the later 427 racing cars, and it was possible to buy this bodywork with no cutouts for sidepipes, to be retro-fitted to existing Cobras. The aluminium body that Howard acquired has no known history at all, but its rear arches look spot on for a genuine 427 body, and the bodyshell itself, when he bought it, was definitely old enough for the unprotected aluminium to have gone white and hard with age.

So it's quite possibly a genuine replacement body that was never fitted. The only visually unconvincing part is the bonnet scoop, which has a rather square and unblended look: as it turns out, Howard didn't get a bonnet with the 427 body, and the bonnet scoop is his own design.

Underneath the body is a chassis that is unashamedly modern. The Metaline packs a semi-ladder, semi-spaceframe chassis under the Cobra shaped skin. It's difficult to see much of the chassis, as every available space in the car is jampacked with stuff, crammed in amongst the extra triangulations that stiffen the whole car up. The inner wings behind the front wheels are full of speakers, and the door hinges are mounted both to the chassis and to the bodywork, so the whole structure adds to the overall stiffness.

The boot contents are further evidence of attention to detail, with a flat floor over the shaped spare wheel well, a trimmed box for the battery, a lined underfloor tool tray, interior lights, and even little leather trimmed boxes to tidy up the tail light wiring as it protrudes into the boot space. There's still loads of room for a dirty weekend's worth of squashy bags, however.

The real distinguishing feature of this car, and the thing which for me makes it different to all the others, is the sidescreens. Okay, lots of Cobra replicas have sidescreens, but there are sidescreens and sidescreens. These are sliding glass sidescreens, in a leather trimmed steel frame. The frame is firmly fixed to the door, and the angled metal at the front steers the sealing strip precisely into place against the windscreen frame. This means no draught, no wind noise, and no rainwater creeping round the edge of the screen and dripping all over your legs, which is a little treat provided by every other Cobra I've ever driven. Luxury indeed.

The heater is rather an ambitious affair, designed specifically for the car rather than adapted from Minis or whatever. The list of tasty heater items starts with the heater control plate. This is a metal casting created for the car, although paradoxically it's so slick it looks as though it came out of a production car. The radius of the edge of

The Metaline has been tested at Millbrook up to 150mph. Must be some amazing experience from the driver's seat. For most of us a more sedate blast through the countryside should suffice.

the plate matches the radius on the dial bezels, which is rather flash: not that anyone would notice, but that sort of thing all adds to the general feel of the car. There's a recirculating function to the heater, which means the cabin air is whizzed through the heater twice, so you get a real blast of cabin heat when you want it. With the roof off, the sidescreens up and the temperature below zero outside, you could still drive the Metaline in reasonable comfort, certainly when compared to most replica Cobras.

The wiring loom is a bit of a novelty, and is a modular electronic affair. The loom in the demonstrator was made across the bench from the loom for Nigel Mansell's car, so it's all very high tech, with rather stiff wires and shrink fit outer coverings over a big single cable running through the car. Everything goes to precisely the correct place, and the bits of loom snap together through the various bulkheads. There's no shortage of electrics in this car, compared to most replicas, so the simpler the better. You can even specify gold couplings for the loom. Nigel apparently went for those, but Howard thought he could probably do something more useful with the grand or so extra that it would have cost.

The bumpers and overriders are actually bumpers, rather than expensive and rather vulnerable bits of trim bolted to the chassis: they're mounted on rubber, so they will absorb parking speed impacts or high speed collisions with Fiat Unos. The general construction of the car seems to be quite strong too: one of them was overturned into a Norfolk ditch, and had to have a new screen, a new boot lock and some minor body repairs. But then we've come to expect Cobra replicas to have the strength of small trucks, as every prang you hear about has the same sort of result.

The aerial costs £125, which seems daft at first. Why bother with that when you can get one for a tenner? However, it is simply the best aerial you can get, and when you turn the stereo on you can just hear it automaticking quietly out of the body. One of Howard's customers thought it was an absurd amount of money, and said leave it off the car. The same chap was having an Aston Martin restored, and when he took a really good look at the aerial supplied by Aston Martin, he rang

Left: Interior is familiar but understated. Thin edges to the fibreglass faithfully replicate the aluminium of the original. Below: Perhaps only the slightly square bonnet scoop lets this example down.

up Howard and said put the posh aerial in the Cobra, please, and, um, could I have another one for the Aston as well?

The suspension is based on the ubiquitous Jag bits, but with a few differences. There are custom anti-roll bars front and rear, and the steering rack is a story all on its own. The rack company Howard was talking to originally shortened the rack to suit his track width by cutting a bit off the end on one side of the rack. This meant lots of steering was available to go right, but not nearly enough to go left. Howard felt that he would have a bit of trouble selling this concept to his customers, and in any case didn't have a great deal of confidence in people with that sort of approach to engineering.

In the end, he finished up with an almost aircraft quality rack, with the slop measured in thousandths of an inch rather than in millimetres. However, you really don't want to know what they cost. The mounting of the rack took some time, as there is one exact position in the chassis which gives the optimum performance from the rack in terms of bump steer, precision, weight and general feel. It took some time to find this, as ultimately the only way to do it is to charge round the same road circuit, with the rack being shimmed, repositioned and secured before each trip.

The engine is designed to be whichever American V8 takes your fancy, and the one fitted in the demonstrator is an original 428CI Ford. This is the direct descendant of the 427CI V8 which gave the 427 Cobra its name, and the one in Howard's demonstrator is basically standard, but has been carefully rebuilt. It's been balanced and so on, but still remains essentially standard. After all, if it'll power the car up to 150 MPH, it's probably powerful enough, innit?

Howard knows the car does 150 MPH because he had it tested at Millbrook. As he puts it, it was "... an experience which is not one to forget but not one necessarily to be repeated."

The chap who was testing it was not just driving it at 150 MPH, he was sprawling comfortably in the driving seat, looking around and admiring the cabin fittings, very impressed with the lack of draughts from the sidescreens. And poor old Howard was sitting beside him twitching, and thinking for God's sake keep your eyes on the road.

I didn't drive the Metaline at 150 MPH, but I did go for a little spin around the East Anglian flatlands. The stonking torque provided by any decent sized V8 makes the car relaxing and comfortable for cruising around looking for photo locations. You don't need to bother

Hood and side doors rarely keep out the weather on a Cobra replica, however they do on the Metaline.

changing gear at all, except to listen to the fab noises that gearchanges conjure from the exhausts. The Muncie four-speed box fitted to this car is quite a nice box, and easy to use. The top-loader Ford box can be a bit of a pig, with an awkward change that needs a firm hand and attention paid to double de-clutching, but the Muncie just snicks in and out of gear, no bother.

The twin side exhausts fitted to the Metaline offer a pleasant compromise, with a quietish chuffling and lots of bass most of the time, but a bit of a snarl kept in reserve for when you feel like putting your foot down. There is a serious stereo fitted to the car, and the sidescreens keep the wind noise down, so there is some point in having a stereo. If you've got serious sidepipes and no roof or sidescreens on, you have to turn the stereo up so loud you get a headache by the time Kylie gets halfway through "I should be so lucky."

Something to avoid listening to in fast cars is the opera Carmen. The crescendos are so effective that you tend to find yourself getting carried away with them, and I nearly topped myself on the way to Brighton once by going round a corner about forty miles an hour too fast, purely because I was listening to Marilyn Horne giving it some stick with the Royal Philharmonic. However, I digress.

The basic body/chassis kit to start a Metaline 690 is around £4000, but the final cost will be up around £20,000 to £30,000. It is after all a very highly finished car. The design of the building of the car shows evidence of the same approach as the interior: every last nut and bolt is organised, and is supplied in packages that relate to various parts of the build. You can buy it piecemeal and introduce your own ideas, of course, but the path of least resistance is to go along with Howard. Still, that high level of detailed organisation would probably make a Metaline easier to build than most.

Chapter 12

AMERICAN CONTEMPORARY

The imported Contemporary Cobra from New York is about as close to the real thing as most of us are ever likely to get: Iain Ayre went to American Speed Specialties for a looksee.

JIM BLACKBURN AT AMERICAN SPEED IS A COBRA man from way back, and looks after a real one as well as importing high quality replicas from the States.

The Contemporary duplicates the Cobra chassis to the extent of copying its massive round tube main front-to-back chassis beams: in the Contemporary chassis these are a stonking 4" in diameter. The engine sits on top of the chassis beams rather than in between them. With a huge 460 cubic inch Ford V8 in the car, there's still a surprising amount of room in the engine bay, with no need for any extra bulges in the bonnet, and the headers are well clear of any obstructions. There's no upper framework to the chassis in the engine bay, which leaves the whole thing uncluttered and quite empty looking.

The original engine bay liner in aluminium has simply been duplicated in GRP, and the radiator follows

Dedicated to faithful reproduction, the Contemporary is desperately close to the original, even down to the real knock-on wheels.

the example of the AC Cobra as well: rather than complicated arrangements and angled radiators, there is a huge radiator right at the front, going right across the car. Again this helps to leave the impression of a neat and spacious engine bay. Development continues in the details: the latest improvements to the breed are drain cocks and bleed valves for the radiator. Neither of them important in themselves, but both of them are indicative of an attitude.

The bodywork is one of the most accurate replicas available. As Contemporary's Monty Gatti is an old mate of Carroll Shelby, it seems likely that the moulds were taken straight from a real 427. The body is also dead tough, and Jim's party trick involves jumping up and down on it just to make the point. (Before it's been painted, this is.)

The body is particularly impressive in the way the cockpit edge is rolled over, as it looks exactly like worked aluminium. The detail that I liked best of all was the way the edges of the air ducts in the front wings are thinned right down, again to look like metal bodywork. Without feeling the bodywork, you really can't tell by looking at the body whether it's the real thing or not.

There are lots of pilot holes dotted around the body

Top: Daytona Coupe is another Contemporary triumph of replication although it is also frighteningly expensive. Above: Not that the 427 is exactly cheap.

to tell you where to drill, and even the slots for the windscreen are ready cut out, which indicates considerable confidence in the precision of the kit's manufacture.

Doors, boot and bonnet are pre-hung on steel frames, and the panel fit is rather better than most production cars. The body is bolted on with eight large bolts, and can be removed within an hour or so. There

Only a handful of Contemporary Cobra replicas exist in the UK, making them possibly even rarer than the original. Now there's a thought!

are no visible hinges on the body at all, and all the brightwork is made in stainless steel.

The wheels are 16" Halibrands. Actual Halibrands, rather than replicas. This means they come with their own quick-release knock-ons and their own pin drives, and they cost a grand a set. The tyres are Z-rated, so they're okay up to 180mph. Which is certainly rather faster than the speed rating on my sphincter. The brakes are Willwood items rather than the more usual Jaguar, and the shock absorbers were developed by Koni in the States specifically for the car.

As you can imagine, none of this is what you might call cheap. To make it even more exclusive, Jim Blackburn will not supply a Contemporary kit to anyone who plans to put a Rover engine into it, any more than he would countenance putting a Rover engine in a real Cobra. He doesn't want to see any Contemporary Cobras on the road unless they'll do the company and the kit justice.

Assuming you use all new parts and fit a 460CI Ford V8 with a Doug Nash 5-speed, the Contemporary will cost you some £25,000 if you build it yourself. You could bring this down to about £22,000 by using a 351 Windsor and a T5 box, or you could go the rebuilt 427 route and spend around £30,000. Because of freight charges, the most economical way to start a Contemporary is to order the Delux Home Builder option, which contains everything except the engine and box, back axle, propshaft, suspension and wheels. "Everything" in this context includes most of what you would usually buy as extras such as instruments, interior, screen, hood, sidescreens and so on. The leather seats, with the historically correct number of box pleats on the squabs, are included in this, as is the steering wheel, with the correct nine rivets on the boss.

Jim Blackburn sees the Contemporary Cobra as the third and top level of replica Cobra ownership. You might start with a budget car built from a Cortina or whatever, then graduate to a Jag-and-V8 car. When it's time to reach up close to the real thing, give American Speed a call.

Chapter 13
DOUBLE VISION

Whilst Steve Carr and Geoff Payne may not be brothers their Classic Replicas Vipers are most certainly identical twins. Ian Stent charts the story.

When two old school friends decided they both wanted a Cobra replica the scene was set for an amazing case of double vision. Steve Carr runs his own auto shop, Carr Automotive Engineering, so he certainly had the technical knowledge to put a kit together while Geoff Payne was, like most of us, simply a Cobra nut. After long discussions about the style of the cars and the standard to which they would be built, it was down to Steve to put the machines together. Almost exactly two years later, these two

Building just one of Steve Carr's immaculate Classic Replicas Vipers would have been impressive, but two is just showing off!

immaculate examples of Classic Replicas' Viper are the result.

When the decision to go ahead with the joint venture had been taken, it was on to deciding which of the many makes should provide the basis for their creations. Steve admits that they didn't do a great deal of searching around and visiting different factories. A ride in Southern Roadcraft's demonstrator was impressive but it was a rolling chassis on display at Classic Replicas' small premises that shone out. As an engineer, Steve could see how strong the Viper ladderframe with steel panelled floor and footwells was, and he also felt confident that he could modify it as and how he wanted. Their cars were going to be special, so he new that whichever product was chosen, it would still require no end of fine-tuning.

Two other factors finally sealed the decision. The first was the willingness of Classic Replicas MD, Ken Cooke, to open up the workshop on a Sunday. He was always helpful on the 'phone and happy to supply details about some of the parts used in the car's construction so that Steve could source them locally to his Wokingham base. Rather more subjectively, Geoff fell in love with the Viper's aggressive front wheel arches. Larger than most other Cobra replicas, the Viper's front arches allow the use of the Jaguar's unmodified front suspension, but it was those outrageous looks that won over this pairing.

With the order made and a delivery date on the calender, Steve set about getting the running gear sorted. Rather than buying a complete donor he sourced two sets of suspension from the nearest scrapyard (remember, throughout the project there would be double of everything!). This was all fully stripped down, shot blasted and then powder coated or stove enamelled depending on the component. From the very word go, the standard of the builds would be to the very highest level.

Both body/chassis kits arrived bang on time, as indeed did everything else that was ordered from Classic Replicas. The chassis were supplied in bare metal and Steve went through two drills and endless drill bits drilling the chassis so that they could be galvanised safely. This process involves dipping the chassis in a hot zinc bath and requires that all sealed tubes be drilled to allow the zinc to get inside and coat all surfaces. If a chassis tube isn't drilled then the hot liquid will heat the air inside the tube to the point when it will expand and distort the tube or

Both cars have these spotless Chevy 350ci V8s under the bonnet. Note how neat the bulkhead panelling is. It gives the engine bay a beautifully neat and simple appearance.

cause it to explode! Still, the process went without a hitch and the fully weather protected chassis went back into the garage.

From here the mechanical side of the project progressed without much modification. The Viper uses bog standard Jaguar running gear and this all fitted without trauma. Instead of fitting the double coil-over dampers at the back, as per the Jag, Steve opted to use only one coil-over per side in the Viper. The bodywork's considerably lighter than on the donor, so he reckoned this would be more than adequate.

Two brand new Chevrolet 350ci V8 engines soon turned up and were mated to Toyota 5-speed gearboxes. Whilst not built to HO spec, they should be good for around 280bhp and have enough torque to pull over a small tower block.

Throughout the whole project Steve had one major campaign, that of hiding any sort of fastener. The stainless steel engine bulkhead panelling has been meticulously cut to shape and fixed without a rivet or nut in sight. And the same goes for the rest of the car; everything that can be fixed without having a visible

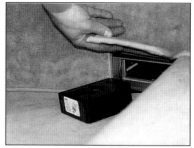

fastener has been. The end result is a fantastic impression of simplicity. Nothing that doesn't have to be seen is in sight and the engine bay looks all the better for it.

With the mechanical side of the project largely complete Steve came to the part of the build he hated the most - fitting the body. Whilst the Classic Replicas's fibreglass main tub fitted onto the chassis without major hiccup, it comes as just a simple skin with all the internal mouldings being supplied separately. These then have to be finally trimmed before being bonded into place. In fact, there were no front inner wheel arch panels at all, but after months of sniffing fibreglass resin, the Viper bodyshell was complete. With all the extra bonding-in, it makes the bodywork extremely strong and there's not a squeak to be had anywhere on either car.

With the main tub in place, Steve began concentrating on getting the various opening panels to fit correctly and with decent shutlines. They're all now millimetre perfect, but it's not come about without some serious fine tuning. Among other things, Steve has replaced all the various hinges and brackets supplied by the company in favour of beefier stainless steel ones. It means the doors are now immensely strong and all visible hinges look immaculate. With further filling and smoothing to the exterior of the bodywork, and all relevant holes cut out, both cars were ready for the local spray shop.

In true fashion, Steve's perfectionist nature meant that the Reading Accident Repair Centre, where the paintwork was being done, was under close scrutiny. Derek Coupe, main paint expert, did the duo proud, with one of the most immaculate finishes I've seen for some time - faultless.

Back at base, energies were turned to the trimming department. Steve's wife, Jayne, was drafted into service with the family's sewing machine to finish off all the edge

Above left: There's a decent size boot in the Viper. Alloy panel can be removed to give access to the Jaguar inboard discs and differential (above). Top: There's even a CD multi changer hidden in here.

trimming on the carpeting. Endless needles later and a sewing machine wheezing its last few breaths of life, both cars were completed.

At each point when a new stage of the build approached, Steve and Geoff would sit down and discuss exactly how they wanted a particular job to be completed. Hours were spent with a dashboard blank fiddling around with cardboard cut outs to find the perfect position for all the gauges and switches. Whilst the Cobra shape was important to the duo, there was never any intention to replicate anything beyond the external curves. Engine bay and interior were built up to the standards which Steve and Geoff set themselves and not to any photographic records of the original '60s muscle car.

You'll have noticed from the photographs that the dash is veneered wood, and one has to say that it really looks pretty damn fine. Of course, you won't see any screws holding it in place, in just the same way as you won't see any hinges on the glove box that Steve's designed. Immaculate with a capitol 'I'.

Steve reckons he's spent at around 40 hours per week for the last two years working on these two masterpieces. That equates to over 4000 hours, but from the moment I set eyes on both cars one can begin to understand where the time has been spent.

Both cars are, quite literally, identical. Right down to the little oddments' tray on the top of the central tunnel, you'd be hard pushed to tell the two cars apart. The attention to detail is evident wherever you look. Open the bonnet and there's a little locating lug to ensure that it remains in exactly the same place when it's closed, with an even shutline at all times. Inside the boot, the CD multi-stacker (Yup, there's over £1500 worth of identical hifi in both of these cars) is hidden under a little flap of carpet, while a stainless steel panel can be easily removed to give access to the notoriously awkward to service inboard Jaguar disc brakes.

Back in the interior, there are speakers of all sizes hidden in every corner you look. There's a fully plumbed in and ready to rumble security system in these cars, too, just as one might begin to expect. And there are more details to admire on the outside of the bodywork. Those vents on the side of the front wings aren't supplied by any Cobra replica manufacturer; Steve didn't like any of the one's that he saw because none of them had a smooth curve on the individual fins of the vents. So he made up his own and they look terrific (of course, no visible screws holding them in place - but you'd guessed that already, hadn't you?).

Above: Interior has been terrifically well executed and Steve Carr has every reason to be proud. These are two amazing machines.

Neither car had covered over 200 miles at the time of my visit but Steve reports that initial ride and handling impressions are better than he'd expected. Both cars currently run a little high off the ground, and Steve's gradually going to reduce the ride height until he finds the optimum. With an underslung exhaust system, the cars sound encouragingly fruity and, once the rear silencers are replaced with cherry bomb style boxes (a forthcoming development), they should sound utterly gorgeous.

Steve's pretty shy about the final cost of each of these beauties. Buying double of everything has given them the opportunity of getting a few discounts, but the end result still ain't cheap. The affordability of the Classic Replicas Viper has helped, but equally it has caused Steve to do rather more fiddling than one might have expected with a more expensive product. Thankfully, his mechanical know-how has meant the project has produced few surprises and he was more than aware of what he was getting himself into.

Is he happy with the end result? Too right. His double creation has come out exactly as he planned it and it looks like the actual driving experience will be even better than hoped. The Viper body/chassis unit has proved up to the job required of it and the company has provided parts and advice as and when required. It's Steve's fantastic eye for detail and doggedly high standards that have produced these two amazing examples of the Cobra replica breed. They show quite clearly what can be achieved with the right attitude and aptitude and it'll be interesting to see how they get on at some of the forthcoming concours competitions. If you want to make some notes before building your own Cobra replica, may I suggest you keep a sharp lookout for either of these amazing creations at any of the larger kit car shows. You won't be disappointed.

Chapter 14

KING COBRA

Sadly, Unique Autocraft is no more: but during their good years they were responsible for some very nice cars. Peter Allen wanted to own the fastest Cobra replica in the country, and he settled on Unique's Python as an excellent basis for just such a car. Iain Ayre was suitably impressed.

THE STORY OF THIS ABSOLUTELY STUNNING COBRA started several years ago when London businessman Peter Allen asked Roy Howard to build him the quickest Cobra ever. After examining a few different replica Cobra chassis options, they chose Unique Autocraft's Python. This was due in no small measure to watching someone open one of the doors while one corner of the car was jacked up completely off the deck. Or to be more precise, it was more a question of watching someone open *and shut* the door while the car was jacked up off the deck.

Unique Autocraft's Python provided the ideal base for Peter Allen's attempt at producing the fastest Cobra replica in the country.

Below: The interior is deceptively simple. The speedo reads to 220mph, the rev counter has a shift light in it and the ashtray cover conceals the nitrous oxide controls. Not quite your average replica.

The company's general attitude to cars and to engineering was also part of Unique's attraction, as was the accuracy of details on the car such as the shape of the dashboard.

The Allen car is unexpectedly beautiful, with a rich, deep paint job that goes some way towards justifying the £3500 it cost. It's unusual for such a single-mindedly performance built beast to look so gorgeous. Most lethally fast dragstrip cars look pretty daggy and battered close to, but this Python gives few visual hints as to its real purpose and character.

The noticeable differences between this and other Pythons are louvres in the bonnet, three covered mounting holes for the roll-over bar in the rear deck, full harness belts on both sides of the cockpit, and an indefinable air of menace.

Somehow the car is all the more threatening for

being such a beauty: as if you asked Brooke Shields for her autograph and she pulled a gun on you, called you an asshole and blew your head off. Incidentally, rumour has it that the end of the world will come when Brooke Shields' eyebrows finally meet in the middle. Not many people know that.

Look more closely around the car and some other alterations come to light. In the boot, there is a nitrous bottle, a battery isolator and a detachable plate covering the Halibrand quick-change differential. Halibrand is a name that tells you there is no compromise in the building of a car. Even with the dollar at its cheapest, things with "Halibrand" written on them are more expensive than things with "Gucci" written on them, and with good reason: the real 427 Cobras used Halibrand wheels, and that was not just because they had nice shiny spinners on them.

The wheel wells inside the boot are panelled in polished aluminium and are radiused to take the 13.5" wide and 28" tall Firestone slicks used when the car is out on the strip.

The drive shafts and universal joints are Hardy Spicer, and the propshaft uses universal joints from a Chevy truck and runs in a protective girdle, just in case.

The rear suspension is not your usual Cobra replica gear, and uses an A-arm by Autopower Services, with a single 400lb spring, soon to be replaced by a 600lb item to add a little more stiffness. The shocks are Spax adjustables, rear braking is by Jaguar discs with AP callipers, and the suspension is solid bushed or rose jointed throughout. The front brakes also use Jaguar vented discs, with Alcon aluminium racing calipers, which are capable of hauling the beastie down from serious speeds quicker than a bundle of used fivers disappearing into a politician's back pocket.

The chassis remains basically standard, apart from a little extra gussetting and strengthening of each weld, and a pair of extra stiffening bars that run from the dash hoop forward to the front of the chassis. Moroso solid engine mounts mean that the engine block itself helps to contribute to the stiffness of the whole car.

The gearbox is special too. It's a four-speed manual G & G, with the outer casing and tail housing made of double thickness T6 aluminium, a steel girdle and billet shafts, a roller first gear, Doug Nash cogs and a shifter by Hurst. The clutch is a twin 10.5" plate Borg and Beck/Long combination, with a Lakewood scatter shield fitted, just in case.

The heart of this beast is its Roy Howard engine, and it's rather special. The specifications sound like a roll call for every top tuning name in the States. The engine is a 454 cubic inch Chevrolet big block, bored 30 thou oversize, balanced and blueprinted, with ported aluminium square-port heads, Moroso valves, an Iskendarian roller cam and Crane roller rockers. Copper head gaskets separate the heads from the block with its 11.5:1 forged pistons and Chevrolet 7/16" rods.

A Pete Jackson gear drive keeps the top end all in order, and the Moroso aluminium water pump and rocker covers save a few extra pounds in weight. The crank is forged and the oil pump has been uprated, and the low profile sump is baffled and screened. The inlet manifold is very carefully matched to the cylinder heads, and the Holley 850 double-pumper carb is fitted with Weber power plates. The neatness of the plumbing for the nitrous oxide injection system, and all the shrouding and panelling inside the engine bay, are a credit to Roy Howard's metalworking skills.

Who'd suspect there's a 640bhp V8 under the bonnet (and that's before the nitrous is switched on!)? For all the world this looks like just another Cobra replica.

The rest of the details are up to the same exacting standards as the engine itself: fuel pumps are Holley racing items, and the twin-point racing distributor, 6T ignition box, rev limiter and automatic ignition retarder for the nitrous are all a matched set supplied by MSD. The HT leads are Mallory 8mm copper, the switchable high output alternator is an Accel: all the braided piping under the bonnet is either Russells or Earls braided stainless steel.

The exhausts were custom made by Unique, and consist of 2" into 4" stainless steel sidepipes, with removable silencers for the drag strip. Or just for the hell of it, for that matter. Cooling, pretty crucial with a monster engine like this in a crowded engine bay, involves a special radiator by Serck, and twin 12" electric fans.

So what's the result of all this hard work and serious chequebook wrestling?

640 BHP.

Yes, that's right, six hundred and forty. Of course, the Nitrous adds another four hundred or so, and that's when it really starts cooking. 1000BHP? No, you're not getting blurred vision, although you would if you poked the throttle pedal in first. Are Peter and Roy satisfied with this? No, not yet. It's quite nippy, but it's not fast enough. On order is an aluminium

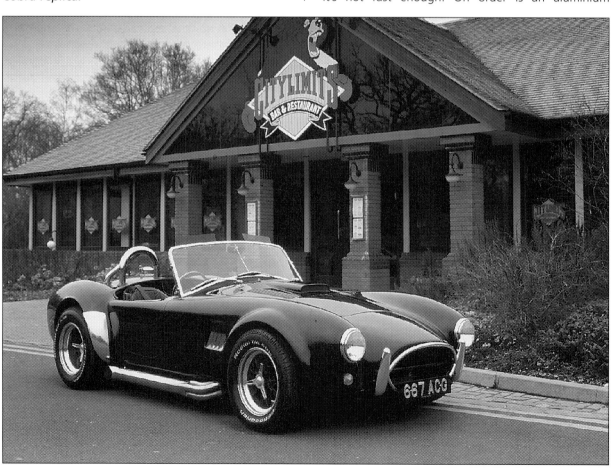

Chevrolet block of some ten litres capacity, which will be given a similar treatment to the current 454. This will then give an estimated 800BHP. That's without the Nitrous, of course...

The current engine will be used to develop and tune all other aspects of the car. Once fully sorted, it is expected to top out at about 220 MPH. Peter plans to run it on the road with full weather gear, but on the strip with no screen and a tonneau fitted. The bar you can see on top of the passenger door is to mount the tonneau and to keep it in place at absurdly high speeds, hence its fairly robust construction.

Under the car's nose is a discreet spoiler, which combines with the aerofoil in the grille mouth in an attempt to keep the front end down on the deck. It's worth remembering that the original Cobras were a good bit short of the 200 MPH barrier because of their buffalo aerodynamics: it took a body change to the Daytona Coupe shape before they really got to silly speeds.

The interior with its restrained black leather seating does not at first sight shout "This is a real mad bastard of a car." The rev counter has a shift light in it, and settings for a rev limiter. The speedo goes up to 220 MPH, and somehow you know that unlike many other 220 MPH speedometers fitted to Cobras, this one's completely serious. The chrome ashtray cover (ashtray? what's he on about?) actually conceals the switches for the nitrous oxide system and the plumbed Halon gas fire extinguisher system.

The ashtray sits atop a transmission tunnel wide enough for a camping holiday, but this is to some extent camouflaged by the neat carpeting in which the tunnel is trimmed. The steering wheel is Moto-Lita, fitted with a turned alloy centre cap and a Cobra badge, rather than the more usual plastic centre. The screws on the steering wheel have been replaced by Allen screws as well, which is a nice detail touch.

The gear lever, far over to the rear and to the left, sports a wooden ball on top, and a line lock switch to lock up the front brakes for warming up the back tyres.

Roy fires up the engine to drive the car to the photo location, and there is much whirling of the Tilton starter. There have been many fiddlings with the carb needles to squeeze the max horsepower out of the engine, and the final balance has not yet been reached: it's sulky and obstreperous. There are one or two muffled explosions inside the exhausts, then a blurt or two of dirty smoke, and suddenly the engine erupts into a shattering roar, causing everyone inad-

Above: This is what it's all about. A 454ci Chevy bored 30 thou oversize and given every tuning goody you can think of. We're talking 1000bhp with the nitrous in full swing.

vertently to step back a pace.

The exhaust pipes have to be negotiated carefully on climbing in, as they will set your 501s on fire given the slightest encouragement. The headers have been wrapped in heatproof material, reducing the engine bay temperature by an estimated 80% and improving the gas flow no end, but in the process making the sidepipes so hot that you can still warm your hands on them half an hour after you've switched the engine off.

The monster rumbles out into the road, with Roy treating it gingerly: this sort of engine has to be warmed up gradually. It's running very roughly because it's cold and because the cams are lumpier than school custard, but it soon settles down as it warms up. The ride is unexpectedly smooth, and you wouldn't think it had solid engine mounts.

The plugs are still a bit fuelly and misfiring a little, so it's given a bit of a rev in second to try to clear them. The car hesitates a little, the barks rabidly and indulges in a lurid power slide down the road. Its contents (ie Roy Howard and your humble narrator) slide to the back of the seats and hit the squabs hard. Roy apologises for the impolite behaviour of the car, but he has no need, as I've got an ear-to-ear grin on my face by this stage. The Python has given me a taste of the its enormous potential, even muffled as it is by having the silencers fitted. It merely requires their removal and a bit more fine tuning before this monster's full explosive potential is unleashed.

One or two smoking-tyre shots seem apposite, so a private road round the back of an industrial estate is found. Inside the car during a take-off, the noise is stun-

ning, as the engine bellows in rage before the clutch is dumped and the tyres start screaming as the Python charges off. The next thing you know, the noise is all off and the brakes are on. The car backs up to the start and does it all again: this time I watch rather than sitting in the car.

Its take-off looks terrifyingly violent, as the gleaming blue projectile hurtles into a blur in thirty feet, with a rich blue cloud of smoke drifting across the road in its wake. However, it feels exhilarating rather than violent, although a stiff neck the next day is a likely souvenir.

Roy is still irritated about the car's earlier unco-operative mood - apparently it's usually only a quarter of a turn on the key before it bursts into furious life - so we get a promise of another day's entertainment, at the dragstrip next time, when the car is fully sorted and at its psychotic best. A real genuine total mad bastard of a car, this one: a ride down the dragstrip on full power would be an experience to rank alongside being licked all over by Kylie.

So is this the King Cobra? Is there a faster one? If you think there is, do let us know and we'll go and play with it.

Chapter 15

BEWARE FAST WOMEN

Gardner Douglas are getting seriously involved in the Retro Sports racing series with a 500 BHP monster GD427, piloted by professional racing driver Heather McAlpine.

AT THE RACE I WENT TO, THERE WAS NO NEED FOR any of the other drivers to beware Heather at all: she started from pole position, and after the first hundred yards, none of them saw her again until the end of the race.

Some of this is down to Heather herself. She was among the first of the professional women racing

Below: Heather McAlpine powers through a corner at Cadwell Park race circuit with not another car in sight.

drivers, and that meant she had to be many times better than all the chaps before she even got a look in. The start of her career came in kit cars, with an O & C Sprint. This got her totally involved, and she just kept bashing away at the prejudice as well as the lap times until she began to get some results that nobody could argue with.

These included success with Formula First, the Willhire series with a Cosworth Sierra, some F3 racing in Japan, and a spell driving trucks. Quick trucks, we're talking about. The quickest truck, in fact: Heather was the British champion truck racer in 1991. Even now,

The win at Cadwell and another wreath to add to the collection. Heather McAlpine has every reason to look pleased with herself.

she can dispose of sausage, egg, bacon, beans and chips, a mug of tea and a slice in 11.26 seconds flat.

The Cadwell Park win was the first clear win for a Gardner Douglas replica Cobra, although Heather took one to a first in class win last year. It's not all down to Heather's skill, though: GD's Andy Burrows got a third place himself at Snetterton last year when he was still more or less running the engine in, and although no slouch as a driver, he's no Stirling Moss. So a good proportion of the win is down to the car.

When I first reviewed the Gardner Douglas car a while back, I said that it wasn't really anything much to do with Cobras at all. The chassis is a very sophisticated tubular backbone affair, which has more in common with the ideas of Lotus and TVR than with the twin drainpipe ladder chassis of AC's cars. Even back then, there was some clever stuff going on, with a most un-Cobra like approach to the problem of balancing comfort and handling. Most Cobra replicators don't really spend much time and effort on innovation in this area, as they're mostly concerned with stonking performance and good looks. However, the engineers' approach that GD have always used resulted in a chassis that was developed for pure handling, and a body that was developed as a separate but rigid unit, attached to the chassis by many rubber mountings, allowing small movements in all directions and damping vibration and harshness to a high degree.

There's also innovation in the body itself, with floors constructed from honeycomb composites, foam filled sills and intrusion bars in the doors. The idea was that the floor should provide immense strength against impact, and if hit really hard, would come up against the lower main chassis beam. In point of fact, someone recently slid a GD sideways into a lamp post, and the theories were all proved correct. The separate mounting of the body also cuts down the risk of stress delamination of the fibreglass due to high frequency vibration, although this is not a problem

Metaline 690 has looks of the sixties but is clearly built for the 90's. Replication goes only so far, beyond which modern standards of motoring comfort and performance take priority.

Above: Metaline looks good from any angle.
Below: These two Classic Replicas Vipers were
built by Steve Carr. Immaculate.

Unique Autocraft may not be around any longer, but this particular example of the Python is just a little bit special. 1000bhp with the nitrous on song!

Gardner Douglas set out to prove that it was the best handling Cobra replica on the market. With Heather McAlpine at the wheel the company proved it in 1995, winning its class in the Retro Sports GT Series.

Below and right: Not all Gardner Douglas cars have to be racers. The GD427 is equally accomplished out on the road. Bottom: They don't get much more outrageous than this example from AK Sportscars. Big stripes, bright paintwork, loud exhaust and in your face!

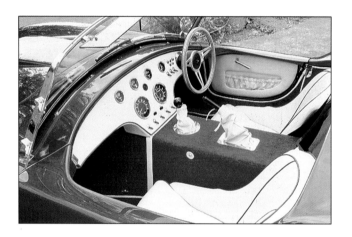

This fantastic looking RAM was built to the customer's specific standards. Chevy power but easy to drive, it's the perfect long distance tourer.

Above and left: Magnum 427 is as low as they come. This customer's car is being built to the highest standards and will be amazing once complete. Below: By contrast, the traditional BRA 289 is the epitome of British restraint.

facing most kit car owners, whose bodywork is thicker than Bart Simpson.

The GD Euro spec chassis is a newish idea: as well as using the traditional Jag rolling gear, you can now use Cosworth diffs, shafts, brakes and so on, with GD tubular wishbones and alloy uprights. This makes the whole car lighter, and allows fine tuning of the suspension: it also allows you to buy the whole set of componentry brand new, and to register the car as new with an "N" registration for 1995/6.

Engines now are a little more sophisticated than in earlier days: the first GD car I drove had a very unusual lightweight Toyota V8, and went very well indeed. The options now include mostly Rover and small-block Chevy, but between those two you can basically get whatever engine you want. A basic EFI Rover new will give you 186 BHP and 32 miles to the gallon, and even with smog gear on, you can still hear the rough chumbling of the V8.

If you're feeling a bit naughty, you can take the Chevy small block up to 500 BHP and still use it on the road: if you go for ally heads and so on, the weight of the 5.7 litre engine isn't too bad either. American engines, particularly Chevies, are so cheap to rebuild compared to European engines: it's always an eye-opener when you actually start ordering bits, and the

smaller bits can sometimes be flown over from the States faster than Ford dealerships can source bits of Sierra.

Talking about 500 BHP engines, that's what there is under the bonnet of the racer. This is the same car about which I waxed lyrical a few years ago in the earlier edition of this very publication, giving it some welly on the old word processor about pink and ice blue skies reflecting off gleaming bonnets. I should coco. The car looks just as good today, but its attitude to life has changed somewhat. It was light, friendly and slick before, and now it's a bit of a bitch, quite frankly.

It's only used for racing now, and has been rebuilt entirely to that end. The engine is a Chevy small-block, but it's one of the heavy duty blocks with cross-bolted main bearings. There is a fully balanced and sorted steel crank, the compression ratio is 11.5:1, the big valve full race head sports roller rockers, and the rev limit is 8000, although only 7500 of those are used on a regular basis.

The car is more or less to standard GD Euro spec,

The Gardner Douglas has been a real force to be reckoned with out on the circuit. It's a pretty damn handy car to have on the road too.

Top: 500bhp Chevy is just a little bit naughty. Apart from the air filter, you won't find any fancy shiny bits in here. This one means business. Above: Interior has little in common with a road going car.

but it retains a Jag diff, which is more or less indestructible. The Scorpio rear end is quite tough too, but the car has stuck with the Jag diff although the rest of the suspension is Euro spec. The rear brakes remain standard, but the discs are grooved: the front brakes use Alcon four-pot calipers and 12" discs. Mind you, it shouldn't be forgotten that every dead Jag comes with a free set of four-pot calipers and big vented discs, and the Jag stuff all still pops on to the GD Jag chassis quicker than you can watch the build video. Yes, they do have a build video: and while Andy Burrows is no Quentin Tarantino, it's a useful idea and in many ways better than a manual.

There's no wimpy nonsense about windscreens and opening doors in the racing GD, although the dark blue colour and the smooth GRP means it still looks quite tasty. The body style was designed originally to use the full width Jag rear end, but with relatively narrow wheels and tyres: the idea was to produce

something between the original fairly restrained 289 Cobra shape and the monster 427 shape with muscles bulging everywhere. The end result is fairly lithe looking, even when it's fitted with racing split rim wheels and fat tyres.

Where you would expect sidepipes or a pair of fat straight-through exhaust pipes, there is a pair of big silencers crammed under the back of the car: the noise regulations are increasingly tough, and to get a car through scrutineering for noise is getting harder. This is a shame, as part of the excitement of racing is listening to a dozen engines screaming and howling round the track. Pretty soon there will be regulations about the smells of hot oil and burnt rubber: next there will be a 30MPH speed limit on all racetracks and we might as well all stay at home.

Still, the silencers for the moment only have to keep the noise down at a specific engine speed, and there are lots of other engine speeds at which the engine still sounds glorious. One of these speeds is where Heather revs it right up as she see the red light on the grid, and as the green flashes on and she dumps the clutch, the deep roar of the Chevy can still be heard above the howling of Jag sixes and the raspy farting of four-cylinder cars.

As the smoke clears, Heather can be seen hurtling away from the rest of the pack, pushing her luck to the limit in the first half mile to create some clear space between herself and the others. If she can open up a decent gap, there is a good chance that the rest of the drivers will be too busy fighting amongst themselves for second place to worry about catching her up. As there are two C-Type replicas doing just that, she is proved right. Ten times she thunders round the upsy downsy and very twisty Cadwell Park circuit: no fuss, no drama, no histrionics, just very smooth and very quick indeed.

Time after time she boots it along the top straight and hauls the car down from a frightening speed to just slow enough to get round the twisty bits and the hairpin, and as the sound of her exhaust fades into the distance, the tangle of Jags and assorted others jam more or less into a line to take the same corner a few moments later in a chorus of screeching tyres and drifts of blue smoke.

Before too long, the final lap comes up and Heather streaks past the chequered flag, to a surprisingly loud chorus of cheers from the crowd. This series is good racing, as the cars are frequently quite close replicas, the Jags in particular. The Gardner Douglas certainly doesn't behave like a racing Cobra, more like a Lotus Elan. (I don't mean the blobby thing, I mean the proper one.) The C-Type Jags look and sound like the real thing, which is probably why the Retro Sports GT series is looking increasingly promising.

It used to be known as the Historic Replica series, but for some reason it was changed: I'm not sure why, as Historic Replica Racing is a pretty accurate description of what you do when you race historic replicas. It's good racing, and I can recommend going along to watch. Particularly next year, because if enough discerning individuals buy my own Jag XK replica kit, I will be racing one myself. However, I don't expect to see Heather in my mirror. Not until she laps me, anyway.

Did I have a crack at driving the GD racer? Yes, I did, for a brief spin round the paddock before it went back on its trailer. Just to get a feel for it. You scramble aboard over the door, then snug down into the seat. The roll cage is effective rather than pretty: a single roll over bar doesn't in reality offer much more protection than a bandanna, but if you find yourself weaseling in amongst a tangle of bars that looks like a children's climbing frame, that will probably do you some good.

No ignition switch as such, just a removable red plastic cut-off key that isolates the whole electrical system in the event of a woopsy. Turn that on, turn on the pumps, poke the starter. The engine is surprisingly co-operative, and just starts with no fuss and idles reasonably smoothly. The gearbox is the industrial strength top-loader four-speed, and even with a Hurst shift it's a bit of a pig, with a very small gate and a firm tug needed to get the message through. Even so, the clutch is the only real reason why this car can't be used on the road.

It's the most evil clutch I can remember: not too heavy, just on or off. It's a small, very butch multi-plate racing-only item, and you simply can't let it in smoothly. When it wants to, it suddenly grabs, and you either stall or boot it and go. The easiest way to get going is to give the engine some revs, and then just let it go and catch the resulting drift as the wheels spin and the back steps out. Of course, the only reason for the existence of this clutch is to get Heather going as quickly as possible, and this the clutch does with clearly demonstrated effectiveness.

If you want your views on women drivers changed, go see a Retro Sports GT race with Heather and a GD427 in it. Mind you, I didn't watch her parking it...

With its racing decals, Heather's car stands out from other Gardner Douglas Cobra replicas that have come to support her. Quite a line up.

Chapter 16

AK YAH

Iain Ayre dons Panama hat and ancient

Dunlops (plimsolls, that is) and pops

orf up the jolly old A1 for a dekko at

the AK427.

ACTUALLY, NEITHER ALAN FREW (THE "A" IN AK) OR Ken Freeman (the "K") are at all posh. The first thing you'd notice about Ken is that he still has a Beatle haircut. He has been told that the Sixties are over, but he's not having any of it. Still, as I myself sport a Roundhead coiffure, perhaps I should be less cavalier about taking the piss.

Below: Built in small numbers, the AK427 has impressed all those who've seen it.

Both A and K are deeply involved in the Cobra Replica Club, which is how they came to be making Cobra replicas in the first place. There have been some dodgy characters involved in the Cobra replica game from time to time, and Ken - at that point just an ordinary customer - bought something fairly unpleasant from one of these types. When the body arrived, Ken looked at it and thought, "I could do better than that mess myself."

Sure enough, he could and he did. At that time, Ken was involved in a small GRP fabrication company, which was just getting off the ground. With a good reputation that quickly spread, the company growed and growed, until the cheques in and out started getting quite substantial, and Ken found himself surrounded by piles of bumf and forward stock requirement budgetary considerations, cash cow options and SWOT analyses and VAT returns.

"Is this loads of fun?" he asked himself.

"Is it bollocks," he replied to himself. He sold out to his partner and went back to making things with his hands, which is what he always liked doing best anyway.

Ken only really meant to make a single Cobra replica for himself, which in the first place is what he did. However, when he took his newly completed pride and joy along to the next Cobra Replica Club meeting, everybody said it was a dead nice body and asked him who'd made it. When they found out he'd done it himself, a good few of them started hassling him to make one for them too.

Even the best Cobra replicas tend to take absolute ages to build, as anybody who followed my own Chevy Cobretti build in *Car Builder* will remember. Nowadays, most of the Cobra kits available are at least buildable, although I have recently seen a very cheap one with a chassis that was visibly out of true. Some of the bodies supplied by the industry's early cowboys were pretty well unusable, at least without serious surgery. Lot of people who had bought kits in the bad old days were now in the position of trying to put the bodies on and were wondering whether their bodies and chassis had

Top: Interior trim is just how the owner wanted it and certainly looks striking with its yellow piping and different dash layout.

genuinely been intended for the same car.

All these people fell upon Ken with glad cries: his one-off mould, still at his old GRP works, was soon steaming from all the bodies it was making, and he began to supply some to the trade as well. To his delight, he began to be asked to build complete cars too, which was a bit like asking me if I'd like to be paid for spending an evening with Jodie Foster. The single

Distinctive double stripe gives this customer's car a really aggresive look that some others lack.

thing that Ken likes best in the world is building replica Cobras, and if he gets paid for it as well, life is pretty well complete.

At a later CRC meeting, a casual remark from Alan Frew, mentioning that he ran a small metal fabrication company, resulted in a long conversation in a corner of the pub. After a few more beers and a few more phone calls, Alan had decided to make a new chassis to suit Ken's bodies - and AK Sportscars was born.

The chassis is a basic, traditional ladder frame, with solid 75 x 50 x 3.2mm main rails. There aren't any steel risers from the ladder: there's a steel scuttle hoop bonded into the body, but the chassis remains very plain: simple but strong.

The bodywork is moulded in only three main sections, cutting down on flashlines and the resultant graft required to get rid of them. Trevira, a man-made fibre that I'm sure they used to make rather nasty suits out of in years gone by, is used to beef up the large flat areas of the body. One of the reasons that less

steelwork is needed above the basic ladder of the chassis is that the boot and bodytub are bonded into the body shell while the shell's still in the mould, and the whole thing is left in the mould until it's had time to cure properly. A pretty strong structure, all in all.

The bodies are fitted to the chassis, and the doors and bonnets are hung before you buy the car, so any body fitting problems would be problems for Ken and Alan rather than for their customers. Most of the other main bits and pieces you need are supplied with the kit, including the radiator frame mounts, the steering rack and arms, shock mount plates, rear tie bars and exchange shortened rear wishbones. Other than shortened driveshafts and the usual goodies, all you then need is the traditional dead XJ6 to supply all the running gear.

The engine options go from Rover V8 up to American small-block: the ubiquitous Chevy 350CI V8 has to be the best value, although 302 and 289 Fords are also worth looking at. AK will cheerfully bung in something different if you want, but you'd probably have to take the engine over to them to sort out the mountings.

There are two conditions of sale: one is that there is no 'deposit now, collect later' system. After bad experiences with the 'deposit' concept when they were customers, both Alan and Ken have decided they don't want to work that way. You order a kit, then when it's ready you pay for it and take it away. If you don't turn up someone else will always buy it anyway, so they don't worry about that. The other condition of sale is that you have to sit in the garden and drink lots of tea until you've been told precisely what is involved in building one of their cars, and until you and they are convinced that you will be able to finish it.

The build manual is in the form of a video, and if you buy that and supplement it with the March and April '95 issues of *Which Kit?* and back issues of *Car Builder* telling you how to sort out the Jag and Chevy bits you need to build a Cobra, you won't go far wrong. Ken has gone to considerable trouble to make sure his life is unpressured and peaceful, so he will always have time to talk over any build problems on the phone.

There were two cars to play with on the day of my visit, representing the extremes of AK cars. A customer called Ben, the proud owner of the yellow and black number, met us at a country pub and insisted on treating us all to lunch: not to any great chorus of objections, I must admit. Ben had the resources to have his car built exactly the way he wanted it, although paradoxically he's too busy earning money to have time to build Cobras himself.

The engine is a Chevy, in a usable state of tune and with a 5-speed manual box. The clutch is a full competition one - i.e. it feels like trying to kick down a brick wall. However, there was little temptation to go thrashing about in the yellow car, as the engine has only done 300 odd miles: better just to leave it in a medium gear and pootle about. Ben is not wee in the same sense that New York's Chrysler Building is not wee, so my relatively small 5'9" ish and 10 stone frame was rattling about in the cockpit somewhat.

However, everything felt well sorted, and there were no noticeable faults in the way the car drove. The detail finish was also pretty good, with a lot of stainless steel on view: this was all fabricated in mild steel first to get the patterns, then duplicated in stainless for the finished items.

The etched glass wind-wings, while not to everyone's taste, are certainly both spectacular and novel. They're the work of a local man, so Ken can point you in his direction if you want something like

that created. The trim in black leather with yellow piping was also very tidily executed, and the piping even extends to the boot interior.

The steering wheel boss is a hand-made job: the same hand can be seen in the rocker covers, and the same attention to detail can be seen in the braiding and polishing of everything braidable or polishable in the engine bay.

The car is just about finished apart from a few adjustments. It was very funny watching Ben, the owner, looking at the sun and then looking at the Cobra and visibly itching to get his hands on it, with Ken, the builder, leaning up against a tree cradling a pint mug and calmly explaining that the car still needed a few bits and pieces tidied up, and that Ben could probably take it away at the weekend. Maybe. With a bit of luck.

The 427 registration is a nice little touch: Ben would ideally have liked a number plate with the letters COB on it, but they cost about the same as the whole of Weybridge these days. The anti-thief system looks as though it cost a few bob as well, come to think of it, with lots of little lights and a beepy item to which you

Chevy engine certainly fills the engine bay and will give the car typically brutal performance when fully run-in.

AK is another top rank contender to add to your increasingly long shortlist of possible Cobra replica purchases.

have to do complicated things in order to be allowed to start the engine. I think as far as protecting my own up-and-coming XK120 replica from thieving vermin goes, I'll chain a Rotweiler to it and then stand just out of range and take the mickey for ten minutes before I leave the car. That should do it, n'est ce pas, mes braves?

Anyway, having spent a while helping to run Ben's

engine in, ambling about in the sunshine with the wind ruffling Ken's Ringo Starr bob and my own quarter inch of receding fuzz, we took the yellow car back to the ranch and pulled out Ken's own car, which serves both as his personal toy and as the AK demonstrator. This is a much more subtle affair, in a tidy dark metallic blue with a plain black leather interior, and it's at the other end of the budget scale from the new yellow monster.

Ken's car is fitted with a friendly old 289 Ford V8, which gives it a respectable amount of grunt without any undignified dramatics. This car has been banging around for a few years now, and reputedly knows its own way to Le Mans: it's wearing well and is comfortable as soon as you plop into the driving seat. It's also quite fast across country, and winds up well for a bit of blattering across Northamptonshire in third and fourth. However, its manners remain polite at all times.

There will never be many AK cars, because Ken Freeman doesn't like the hassle of running companies when they get too big. However, I'd have to agree with the Cobra Replica Club in welcoming rather a good car to the scene.

Chapter 17

A WOLF IN RAM'S CLOTHING

Carroll Shelby has chosen to endorse

the Ram as a replica of the original

Shelby Cobra: if anyone knows what

he's talking about, Shelby should.

Left: Endorsements don't get much better than having Carroll Shelby's seal of approval.

THE REASON FOR SHELBY'S ENDORSEMENT OF Ram's product becomes clear when Ram's Adrian Cocking tells you how Shelby feels about Cobra replicas. There has always been a rumour that Shelby doesn't like replicas, which is not apparently the case. What he doesn't like is poorly engineered copies of an out of date product.

The 427 powered Shelby Cobras were legendary cars, and they were wonderful fun for the time. The chassis design was not exactly sophisticated, and the vast power of the engines was mostly down to their sheer size. The trick was in putting the biggest possible engine in the lightest possible car, and the result was awesome.

However, Carroll Shelby reckons that it was certainly awesome for 1965, but that the world of Cobras should have moved on a bit since then: faithful reproductions of a very old and flawed design don't give him much of a buzz. He probably wouldn't have a problem with the quality of most of the better UK replicas these days, but the closer the replicas are to his originals, the less they interest him.

The Ram he sees as evidence of progress, largely as it has a spaceframe chassis that bears little resemblance to the original double drainpipe. Another element that interested Shelby was the four-wheel-drive Ram that was built a few years ago. As it happened, it wasn't a success. It handled very well indeed, but it was no fun, so it was dropped. Why had Adrian created it, Shelby wanted to know. To see what happened, was the answer, more or less. Anyway, the upshot of all that was that the chassis plate on a Ram 427SC replica now says CSXR and then a number: that's a continuation of the Shelby chassis numbers with the addition of "R" for replica, and it's something rather special.

The chassis under the Ram SC has always been a substantial Adrian Reynard designed round-tube spaceframe, with a very big, wide transmission tunnel and an unstressed bodyshell. There is a

Above: You won't see many replicas with aluminium bodyshells, but Ram can and do offer the service. Below: Just in case you forgot.

DESIGN APPROVED BY *Carroll Shelby*

subframe bonded into the bodyshell which locates all hinges and mounting points on steel, and the whole arrangement then bolts to the chassis through metalastik bushes, which cuts down on vibration. The same steel frame gives good side impact protection as well as locating everything on steel.

Donor for the SC is still the ubiquitous Jaguar, with the usual independent rear end. At the front, Ram use the upper wishbone from the Jag, but substitute their own lower front wishbones. The list of other donor parts reminds you that this kit has been going for ten years, with the wipers sourced from Marinas, the heater from a Spitfire and the steering column from a Mk 1 Escort. However, these parts are all supplied by the factory, so finding them is Adrian's problem rather than yours. In any case, things like wipers and heaters are easily adapted from lots of sources.

Never one to sit still, Adrian has been developing the SEC version of the car, which uses more up-to-date mechanicals with the idea of gaining full low volume type approval and making finished cars. The emissions test is all that's left, and that's something of a formality, as it's a matter of choosing a previously tested modern engine and then fitting the necessary exhaust and catalytic gubbins to your own vehicle.

The SEC drops the Jag as the main mechanical donor, and uses a modern Ford rear end, a mixture of Sierra/Granada/Cosworth that has proven well up to taking a bit of a spanking from big V8 engines. After all, a naughty Cosworth Pinto can be hopped up to kick out 500 BHP, albeit for a limited period of time, and Ford rear ends do not have a reputation for going pop or we would have heard about it by now.

This is not the sort of car that anyone would think about fitting with a Cortina engine, so the choice is between Rover, small block or big block American power. I would always recommend a Chevy 350 small block. Start with 250 or so BHP standard, and you can bolt on another 250 horsepower again, no bother at all. The value of American parts is excellent. I needed to get more than 600 cubic feet of air per minute into my Chevy engine: this would have cost about £1200 in Webers, but in fact cost £120 with a four-barrel Carter. Not as sophisticated as the Webers, but at 10% of the cost, I wasn't wingeing.

The official Ram demonstrator was in Europe on the day of my visit, but there was a rather spectacular recently finished customer car around that needed some test miles on it, so Adrian took me for a spin in that. It's been set up for both of the couple who own it to be able to drive it, so there's a servo on the clutch, and the suspension is set fairly soft. There was no need to demonstrate what the car was capable of at the limit, because I had already played with one on that basis several years ago, and had no complaints.

With this one set up for comfy cruising, it displayed a completely different character, which came out more as we drove it. Let's face it, when you're on the edge round a roundabout with all four tyres shrieking and a big V8 bellowing through the sidepipes, it's difficult to remember to judge the level of vibration transmitted to the body.

However, when you're bimbling along chatting

while a new engine is gently run in, you can take the time to pay attention to that sort of thing. The ride is certainly smooth, and while you can still hear the inboard discs of the Jag rear end, as in virtually all cars fitted with the Jag rear end, you definitely can't feel it. Underfloor exhausts allow a bit of a growl now and then, but the only real noise is the slipstream, and there's nothing anyone can do about that without getting rid of the body shape.

One of the interesting things about Cobras, real or replica, is that the huge gape at the front, combined with the squat, aggressive stance, shifts everything out of the overtaking lanes except Volvos: but then Volvo drivers don't have to look in their mirrors because they're Special.

The T5 gearbox is a lot more pleasant to use than the old top-loader, and offers an interesting combination of gears. American emissions regs and the increasingly tight mileage per gallon demands are so ferocious that some imaginative twisting and turning has been necessary for Ford, GM et al to keep selling cars. The T5 is one of these twists. Essentially, it's a four speed box, but with an additional very high, almost overdrive gear to allow a

Right: Interior of this customer's car is terrific.
Below: A really pretty example of the breed.
Note the twin roll-over hoops behind each seat.

Top: Rams have more than proved themselves in competition. Below: Chevrolet engine in test car was still being run in.

big V8 to achieve good MPG by only turning over at a few hundred RPM while cruising at 55 MPH. This gear is only usable while cruising on flat roads, but it will save a good few quid along the way.

Moving the car around to grab some photos, it was noticeably easy to drive compared to some Cobra replicas. The clutch was nice and light, if a little slow in operation, the engine was prepared to stop and start over and over again without any histrionics, and sensible sized wheels and tyres meant you could turn the steering wheel at parking speeds without having to stop during a three point turn for a rest and a cup of tea. When I think about past occasions, moving one or two Cobra replicas about for exactly the same reason, the Ram was pretty amenable by comparison, certainly when compared to a V12 with a polo mint steering wheel.

Ram have been pretty active in other areas in the last while. They were involved in the Bardahl one-make racing series in France for three years. This did quite well, when you think it was a recession and each car cost £40,000. The cars ran 400BHP engines, dyno tested to be within one or two percent of each other, and there were usually fourteen or fifteen cars on the grid. The Cobra shape's enduring popularity combined with 400 BHP, a lack of racing slicks and no spoilers or air dams made for exciting racing: the Ram cars aren't perhaps as unruly as the real thing, but they're certainly no pussycats. However, the series ended after three years.

The company have recently been involved in prototyping work with Oldsmobile and Carroll Shelby, which is all rather intriguing. Oldsmobile have a marketing problem, which is that all their customers are dying of old age, and nobody under pensionable age wants to be seen in an Oldsmobile. They have been enthusiastically supporting drag racing for ages, but nobody knows about that. You can't necessarily see that a dragster packs an Olds engine, so it hasn't done much for their image.

Chrysler's image is the result of the Hillman Avenger, the Chrysler 180, and ultimately the Talbot Horizon. I objected to the use of the name Talbot in connection with the Horizon and Solara at the time, as I thought the name should have been allowed to die with dignity, not exhumed and misused on those two. Suffice it to say that a few years ago, if you said the word Chrysler, most people's lips would curl. Nowadays, however, say Chrysler and everyone thinks Viper. In a few years, one monster car has changed the whole public image of the company.

Oldsmobile have obviously been looking upon this phenomenon with some envy, and as they're strongly linked with Shelby, we can expect to see something happening in the not too distant future. I have no inside knowledge about the form the car will take, but I can tell you that Adrian shipped one of his cars out to Phoenix, Arizona, to test the possible engine for this new Shelby Oldsmobile whatever.

The engine was based on the North Star engine used in Cadillacs. This is an all alloy four-litre 32-valve four-cam V8, that produces 310 BHP and in a Ram does 32 miles to the gallon. The car did 0-60 in 4.2 seconds, 0-100 in 10.3, and the standing quarter mile in 12.7. The last car they tested there that went faster than that was an AC Cobra. And that 4.2 second time was with an all up weight of 2400 lbs and a set of old racing tyres. The car is not any sort of lightweight, it's just an ordinary prototype.

Putting the engine in was harder than you might have thought, however. The North Star engine was designed to go in sideways, and putting it North-South caused a few headaches. The water pump is now right at the back of the engine and sticks out to one side. Could they bung it on at the front instead? No they bloody couldn't bung it on the front, said GM, it cost $150,000,000 to design it the way it is. Oh well, better change the chassis a bit instead, then.

The other problem was the clutch and flywheel. There are virtually no manual American cars any more, and the engine had never been designed to work with a manual box. The starter motor was in the vee on top of the engine as well, and the problem with that was that the flex plate was only 12" across. For an automatic, this isn't too bad, but for a manual clutch that's not a very big flywheel when you're

Right: Enormous central tunnel straddled by comfortable seats. Headrests are a nice touch and help to modernise the interior slightly. Below: Great car set-up for easy blasting.

planning to wang several hundred horsepower through it by slipping your foot sideways off the clutch. The eight 8mm bolts holding it all together couldn't be changed either. In the end, they used hardened bolts, double dowelled it, clench ringed it and hoped for the best: as it happened, 4.2 seconds to sixty was no bother at all, and the clutch stayed obediently in its housing, although it did get a bit smelly and hot.

That was all with a standard engine, of course. Does anyone seriously think that Carroll Shelby will be able to resist developing the engine from potentially evil to potentially diabolical, before shoehorning it into a car that's far too light for it? That's what he usually does, after all. Let's keep an eye on Ram and see what happens.

Chapter 18

GARDNER DOUGLAS COBRA FOR ALL SEASONS

It would seem that Gardner Douglas has the Cobra replica market pretty much sewn up. Ian Stent takes his pick from three very different examples of the breed.

HMMM...DO I WANT A JAGUAR BASED CAR WITH A Rover V8 or a modern GD EURO car and all-singing Chevy 350ci pumping out the horses like there was no tomorrow? Or perhaps a Jag based car with a Ford 302ci or a GD EURO with a Rover? Choices, choices, choices.

GD427's chassis is a well engineered backbone affair allowing all the mechanical components to be fitted prior to the body going on.

You can see how the prospective customer might get a little befuddled when he makes an innocent visit to Gardner Douglas thinking his choice would be simple.

On our last visit to the company main man, Andrew Burrows, had assembled no less than three examples for us to pick over and briefly sample. The first of these was a customer built Jaguar based car using the ubiquitous Rover 3.5-litre V8 for its power. The second was another customer car using GD's recently developed EURO suspension and a stonkingly powerful Chevy 355ci V8. Rounding up this mighty trio was GD's own new demonstrator using the EURO suspension and a brand new Ford 302ci injected V8 from a Mustang, complete with catalytic converters etc.

Andy Burrows is quite proud of his GD427, and justifiably too, because his Cobra replica is unique in a number of areas when compared to other fake snakes on the market. Up until recently, this uniqueness has been based around the body and chassis construction but with his new suspension designs he has also set new standards for the market to follow.

When Andy came to design his chassis he had a number of important objectives to achieve. Without stating the obvious, strength was one but light weight was another. In order to get a ladderframe chassis torsionally strong it has to be big, and that means weight penalties. Spaceframe construction was another alternative, but a backbone chassis achieved a number of things that would have been difficult to obtain with the former.

A backbone set-up makes assembly during the build-up nice and uncluttered whilst enclosing the drivetrain is a substantial safety cage. Combined with GD's unique body

construction, the chassis can be fully built with suspension, engine and gearbox, wiring, brakes, steering and almost everything else in place prior to fitment of the body. The chassis then acts as a positioning jig for the body, with precise construction tolerances ensuring that it is impossible for the builder to misalign the body on the chassis.

Using a backbone chassis means that the body has to be self-supporting and in order to achieve that you're looking at a monocoque type construction. Front and rear bulkheads become moulded-in structures with a honeycomb sandwich floor and foam filled sills and side panels. Every panel is designed in such a way as to spread loads through the whole structure and reduce the pressure on any one area.

The way in which the body is fitted onto the chassis is also unique. The body is completely isolated from the chassis by special rubberised isolation mounts, of which there are fourteen dotted around the chassis at various location points. There are two main reasons for this method of location. The first is to help reduce feedback from the drivetrain and chassis into the body, so reducing fatigue and increasing driver comfort. The second is to make later removal of the body for any major mechanical servicing firstly possible and secondly easy. Through cunning location of the brake and clutch reservoirs it is, I am told, merely a ten minute job to remove the body and reveal the exposed chassis and

The Gardner Douglas is a more slender version of the typical 427, harking back to earlier 289s. Modern wheels give the company demonstrator a decidedly up to date feel.

mechanicals below. That's an excellent idea.

Up until recently, the only GD427 you could buy used the Jaguar based suspension common to most Cobra replicas and many other exotic GTs and open-tops. The blue car in the pictures is based around this running gear. It has been built by farmer, David Hodgeson, and his aim was clearly the retro look, with full knock-on wire wheels and reasonable profile tyres. I've always been intrigued by the GD body styling, which is slightly different to most 427 replicas you find on the market. But rather than straying from the path of replication it is merely linked more closely to the earlier Mk3 289 Coil Spring Cobra. Perhaps most distinctive are the more slender, less bulbous rear wings.

With the traditional 15" wire wheels from a Jaguar, David's car really looks the part when combined with all the usual Cobra brightwork and traditional leather interior. The paint finish was done locally and is more workmanlike than concours, but the car is used regularly and hard, so that's probably not a bad thing. Under the bonnet nestles the familiar Rover V8 lump which received a comprehensive re-build and mild tuning by David before it found its new home. Clearly it's the mechanical side of things that are this builder's forte and the engine bay is a great example of smart presentation and attention to detail.

The interior also shows signs of David's mechanical and welding skills. There's a beautifully presented floor-mounted handbrake made from all sorts of bits including part of a motorcycle front strut! In operation it's beautifully smooth and refined. The gearbox has been modified to bring the gearlever slightly further forward on the tunnel. Even the gearstick itself is home-made and includes a slick lift-up reverse gear lock-out. Terrific.

David is well over 6' and has repositioned the pedals to give him the correct length. Consequently, for most other people, either the pedals are a little too far away or the steering wheel or a little too close depending on adjustment of the seat. Still, it's not enough to make driving impossible.

Fire up the Rover and two underslung exhausts issue a familiar Rover V8 woofle...aah, this is the life. Out on the road it soon becomes clear that David has wound the adjustable coil-over dampers up quite hard and the car feels a tad harsh over undulating back roads. It's just enough to make long journeys a bit more tiring than they ought to be in a car of this nature. On my return it transpires that the wire wheels have 7" rims instead of the intended 6" ones and with the suspension set softly causes the higher profile Goodyears tend to scuff the

wheelarches over the bumps. It's a real shame that rather overshadows what is clearly a nicely tempered roadster.

The steering, perhaps as a result of the harder suspension and the need to run 25lbs pressure in the tyres due to the fitment of inner tubes, is a bit on the light side for my liking but firms up really nicely in the corners to give that vital feedback needed to push on through the twisty bits with confidence.

Whilst the clutch and accelerator pedal are both light and progressive, the brake pedal is rock solid in operation. There's no brake servo and this is one of around ten GDs supplied with the Tilton pedal box assembly using twin brake master cylinders and bias control front to back. I've normally had nothing but praise for these units but on the GD the brakes, whilst highly effective, are too solid to give the beautifully progressive feel that was clearly evident on the other two cars.

The Rover V8 engine is surely the most commonly fitted unit in the Cobra replica fraternity and on this car was reputed to be putting out around 180bhp. It provided the Gardner Douglas with quite adequate performance without being a shocker, although as the revs climbed above 4000rpm the exhaust note become somewhat harsh rather than raucous. Still, it was enough to give the car a good turn of speed and David's home-made gearlever clicked its way through the 5-speeds with a beautifully classic feel.

Mine was an all-too-brief drive of the car that, due to harsh back roads, sadly highlighted the over-firm set-up imposed by slightly unsuited wheel sizes. That said, the suspension feels well set-up with no nasty geometry shocks to catch out the unwary. The build quality was very high and with the wheel problem solved this will surely be a classy mid-range performer. David reckons he went only slightly over his budget of £12,000 but the level of finish and quality of the donor reconditioning seem to more than justify that sort of outlay.

The next machine I got my hands on was the mighty Chevy 355ci powered beast pumping out a reported 425bhp! Oh boy...this should be interesting.

Andrew Bird isn't new to kit cars. In fact he owned a Brightwheel Viper before building the Gardner Douglas, so he's a true Cobra nut. With the GD427 he wanted something a little special and the first step towards achieving that was to order GD's new EURO chassis. Gardner Douglas only supplies this set-up in rolling

Front suspension of the Euro chassis where the conventional Jaguar components are replaced with purpose designed uprights and wishbones.

chassis form, citing quality control as the main reason for not offering a basic chassis and set of wishbones, so Andrew's build has progressed in a fairly straightforward manner but even now there are still some odd jobs to be completed. You'll notice his car is at the moment devoid of front and rear nudge bars and his will be the only one here to be fitted with a roll-over bar.

This car has also received a paint finish, this time in metallic and to a top quality standard. The interior won't let the side down either, with luxurious carpet, all the usual trimmings and some neat custom made cappings to keep everything up to scratch. That said, I think it's a real shame that the body to chassis location bolts are left visible on the side of the central tunnel (on the Jaguar based car David has hidden them under the carpet). Just how often will you need to take the body off the chassis?

You'll notice that none of the GD427s have the external bonnet latches common to most fake snakes and that's because they are all operated by a more conventional latch method with release situated under the dash in the cockpit. GD boss, Andy Borrows, tries to discourage his customers from using the traditional latches, and also the massive flip-top fuel caps, for two main reasons. Not only are they dangerous in the event of an accident involving pedestrians but (slightly less important) Andy feels they spoil the otherwise smooth lines of the car.

There's not a lot under the bonnet of this car to suggest that it's anything other than a normal Chevy 350ci. But perhaps the huge round air filter was an omen of things to come. Back in the cockpit I immediately fall into difficulties with the large 15"

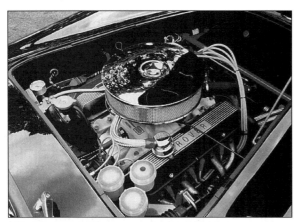

Above: Very tidy engine bay in this Rover powered example. This car was also Jaguar based, unlike the two other cars which had Euro chassis. Below: Injected Ford 302 is an unusual sight in a Cobra replica.

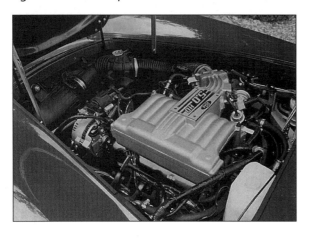

steering wheel. It's simply obstructing my legs and precluding me from getting comfortable. Still, the owner doesn't find it a problem so I'll just have to make do.

The 6-speed Richmond gearbox is solid in action and required a firm hand to keep things on the move. As we drive out into the road I'm immediately impressed by just how well sorted this car is. The suspension is firm but, at the same time, supple enough to absorb the lumps and bumps of a less than forgiving back road. The steering feels beautifully bedded-in, being light yet with perfect balance and feedback. As with the Jaguar based car, it firms up responsively in the bendy bits.

I must admit to having a real soft spot for big American V8s and this one's a real treat. It offers that instantaneous throttle response that is so exciting. Touch the throttle and the car responds immediately, no matter whether you move the pedal half and inch or punch it to the floor. The latter, it must be said, should only be done by the very foolhardy, for with 425bhp available at the snap of a finger, this beast could seriously catch out the inexperienced. Well perhaps not, because GD's

EURO chassis is clearly a master at taming these levels of performance. Rarely have I come across any car that contains such power so well. Even with this monster engine it'll take some pretty heavy handed treatment to unstick the rear tyres.

Fast? Just a bit!

Such is the finesse of the GD EURO set-up that even after just fifteen minutes I find myself pushing this wild thing through twisting corners in a way one wouldn't dare try in other cars after a week. That is surely, in part, due to the reduced unsprung weight of this car when compared to any Jaguar alternative. STATUS manufactured alloy uprights and GD's own wishbones have replaced the cumbersome items normally employed from that mighty British cruiser, the Jag XJ6. Also playing its part must be the more adjustable suspension geometry allowed by this set-up over the more fixed Jag alternative. One thing's for certain, it makes the Gardner Douglas a hugely capable performer.

The brakes, this time GD's own set-up, are more progressive than the Tilton variety used in the Jaguar car although they're still hard and require a firm positive action from the driver. The six speed gearbox takes a bit of getting used to. The gears are extremely close together but once mastered will no doubt be a real joy to use. Sixth gear is unbelievably high and at 70mph the engine is almost idling at less than 2000rpm! Still, with 425bhp under your right foot, this mammoth machine will happily pull away cleanly from under 1500rpm. Awesome stuff.

Finally we come to Gardner Douglas' own new demonstrator. This is the only car here with a coloured gelcoat finish. And what a finish it is, too. A quite excellent moulding that has produced a gelcoat with a beautifully smooth finish and deep lustre.

Under the bonnet we find Ford's latest injected Mustang 302ci V8. It certainly looks unusual situated under this bonnet and is clearly aimed at markets abroad. The car's fitted with catalytic converters and much of the other gubbins normally associated with such things. In this utterly standard form it's an engine pumping out an utterly respectable 245bhp and 285 lbs/ft torque.

This car I find the easiest in which to obtain a comfortable driving position. A sensible sized 13" steering wheel makes for loads of knee room and, with the pedals in their standard position, I'm quickly at ease. The gearstick is canted over at a rather funny angle but falls neatly to hand. In action it has a rather typically vague production car feel about it. A bit disappointing.

The demonstrator is running slightly softer springs than the other EURO car and these and the dampers were still bedding in during our visit. The ride is definitely on the soft side - just a little too spongy, but the steering still has that positive feel to it and the brakes are just as communicative as on the other car. With just ninety odd miles on the clock it is clear there are still a few minor bugs to sort out. Apart from allowing the springs and dampers to settle, the rear toe-in setting was a little array, causing the back end to get a little lively over the more uneven back roads. Adjustment is extremely easy, and Andy immediately altered it on my return to the workshop.

What a shame it hadn't been spot-on for my drive because otherwise this was a real beauty. In typical injected style, the 302 produced power in a refined and smooth torque curve that was utterly manageable but also highly effective in hustling the Garner Douglas along in great style. Following the Jaguar based car back to GD's unit, I could reel-in the lesser powered machine at will on the straights while only the oddities of this car's rear suspension set-up forced me to tread a little more wearily through the bends.

At the end of the day I found this Gardner Douglas visit a really interesting exercise. These were three utterly different cars all emanating from the same manufacturer.

But which to choose? Put quite simply, cost may well be your deciding factor. Jaguar based cars have been put on the road for as little as £10,000 while most will be looking at nearer £12-15,000 (GD's fine coloured gelcoat finish can help reduce that). The EURO option is a rather different kettle of fish. If you order the basic rolling chassis less engine and 'box and build up from there you may get something on the road for under £20,000 while if you order a complete rolling chassis and then a complete body pack (pre assembled) you'll be paying upwards of £31,000. Quite a difference over the Jag based car.

If the price hasn't helped you make up your mind then you need to look at the merits of each option. Let's not forget that almost all other Cobra replica manufacturers use Jaguar mechanicals as the basis for their cars. They do this for the simple reason that the Jaguar parts are robust and do the job of carrying around a Cobra-like bodyshell quite admirably. Not just that, some are very good cars indeed and the Gardner Douglas option must be up there with the best of them. Its price is also very competitive, too.

As a build-up prospect the GD (in both guises) must also score very highly as I'd imagine it's one of the more straightforward to construct. The ability to almost totally build the car with the body and chassis split must really help matters.

By comparison to the Jag based car the EURO option has very few competitors. Certainly none that we are aware of offer a backbone set-up while perhaps only one or two others run non-Jaguar based suspension.

Interior is typically immaculate, with loads of leather and quality carpet.

I wouldn't hesitate to say that this set-up is clearly very capable and delivers a superior ride and handling to most Jaguar based kits. The suspension design, as a point of fact, offers more geometry adjustment that you can hope to achieve using Jaguar components.

If you're a hard driver, who likes to get the most from his cars, then the EURO unquestionably offers the edge in terms of shear composure, steering feel and awesome brakes. It's a car in which you can feel totally confident. I wouldn't go the all out 425bhp route, damn good fun though it is. Far more user friendly and offering bags of bhp and torque is the injected Ford 302 of the company demonstrator. The EURO offers the owner a top-fight driving experience with all the splendour and presence that comes from that classic shape. If you've got the dosh, you could do a lot worse than putting it into a GD427 EURO.

Sadly, the bottom line will probably be that few of us can actually afford the EURO package so it's just as well that Gardner Douglas still offer the Jaguar option. For me, this car's main plus points are it's apparent ease of build, quality of gelcoat finish and overall affordability. For a comparatively middle-range sum you should be the owner of a Cobra replica to match rather more expensive machines. One thing's for sure, it really ought to be on your test drive list when you come to make a decision.

Chapter 19

DO YOU FEEL LUCKY, PUNK?

The Magnum has more or less the same destructive power as Dirty Harry's blunderbuss, and it will also blow your head clean off.

THE MAIN REASON WHY MAGNUMS LOOK MORE EVIL than any of the other replicas about the place is that their standard ride height is 4", compared to the average 8" of most cars. This is achievable not least because they have a completely flat undertray. Don't you usually find that sort of thing on racing cars rather than road cars? Quite.

As Magnum's Mike Broad says, there's very little connection between this car and the AC Cobra, except that the outer body shell looks similar. Underneath the

Lower than a very low thing, the Magnum has all the presence of its handgun namesake.

shell is a very high performance vehicle, with the chassis designed by Mike from scratch.

The chassis is a backbone spaceframe, with outer rails to give some side protection, and with detachable and disposable subframes mounted at either end to provide crumplezones. The central section is made out of round section seamless steel tubing, and is not intended to deform. There are integral roll over bar mountings for single or double bars. As you can gather from this, the car is intended to be used in anger, whether on or off the track.

The suspension shows the same lack of compromise, and is mostly fabricated. At the front, fully adjustable wishbones are mounted on urethane bushes and rose joints, with either Koni or Spax adjustable coil-overs. The rack is Capri, which provides the right steering geometry with a choice of ratios depending on the size of your biceps, your steering wheel and your bottle. The rack is mounted on solid ally billets, and a very tasty little touch is the fully height adjustable rose-jointed trackrod ends.

These mean you can set your ride height, camber

and castor just where you like it, then you can alter the height of the trackrod ends to dial out any traces of bump steer that may result from your settings. This is in marked contrast to the last of the TVR kit cars of the early Seventies, in which the way to deal with bump steer was to keep your thumbs well out of the way of the steering wheel spokes.

The front uprights are Jaguar, which come as standard with big ventilated discs and four-pot calipers: Magnum can also supply aluminium calipers to fit, and this would make a significant difference to the unsprung weight. Jaguar's calipers weigh about as much as Fiat's engines.

The rear suspension is up to the same standard, with wide and stable fabricated tubular wishbones, and a fabricated upright to take Cosworth/Scorpio hubs and disc brakes. The shafts are also shortened Cosworth, but there is a choice of diff. You can either continue with the Cosworth theme, or you can have a Jag diff. I'm not sure which is the best option, as both are pretty well bombproof. The Cosworth is limited slip as standard, and I know someone who has a 500 BHP Sierra running through one of those diffs: he's been ill-treating it for some time now without breaking it.

For ultimate differential beef, Magnum have just fitted a car with a diff based on a Jaguar casing, but with American ratchet or locking internals. These are super tough, and apparently don't snatch the way you would expect. They are noisy, but like superchargers, American V8s and the Rolling Stones, some things are just naturally pretty damn noisy but it's just what we want to hear.

There are additional anti-roll bars available for both the front and the back ends, which are made out of T45 aircraft quality material: but the performance of the standard suspension means that hardly anybody bothers to fit them.

The brakes are also rather obviously track orientated rather than road. The system involves an entirely Kunifer/Aeroquip plumbed, split front to back system, with two separate master cylinders. The bias is first coarsely adjusted by choosing the bore of those cylinders, then a fully adjustable balance bar is set up just the way you like it. Finally, the pedals are also adjustable. With a notably light car, there's no need at all for a servo. Mind you, I see servos as optional anyway: I liked the feel of the Dax big-block demonstrator with no servo when it first came out, and I'm no muscleman. As Mike says, if the brakes feel too heavy you can always use cheap soft brake pads to cut the pedal weight.

The floor and panelling on the chassis is hard NS2 aluminium sheeting, and the tunnel and engine bay areas are double skinned and insulated: having a 450 BHP Chevy lump in your lap can get a bit toasty in a July traffic jam. The seat mounts are tubes welded

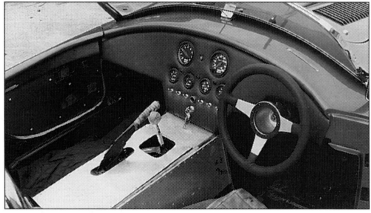

Top: Bonnet is an aluminium affair - there will be no compromises with this customer's car once it is finished. Below: No real interior yet, but who cares when it's this mean?

across the chassis, to which the seats are bolted without runners. You just make up your mind where you want to sit, and bolt them down. The seats themselves are fabricated by Magnum from steel and wood, and have very low squabs. You sit in a Magnum rather than on it, which also means the screen can be raked at a sharper angle to cut wind resistance.

The body is a single skin affair, with internal bulkheads fitted. The shell is reinforced with 30% Kevlar, which is as light as an Orvieto spritzer and as strong as Special Brew. It's not bonded on, but bolted at 18 points: along the sills, front and back, and at several points high up in the chassis. The oldest Magnum has served seven years and 30,000 miles with no stress cracking, so the system works. Panels are all double skinned and mounted directly to the chassis steelwork, and there are generous lips around the body apertures to keep the weather at bay. Although even if the boot is waterproof, I can't believe the cockpit is: if it rains on a Cobra, you get wet. The water always creeps round the corners of the screen and dribbles down on your legs. There are certain circumstances in which I quite like having my legs dribbled on, but driving cars isn't one of them.

The car I was supposed to go and look at for the purposes of this publication belongs to a Magnum customer, who was keen to show it to me. Unfortunately, it got stuffed in Holland a couple of weeks ago. As demonstrators go, it's done its job, however: the front crumple frame has already been repaired and sent over, the front end of the body is being repaired and the owner was unhurt.

The bluey green car in the photos just happened to be around, and it is as good a salesman for the brand as any Magnum, even if it's not finished. There's only really the trim and odds and sods still to go, and the character of the car is pretty well established. Or rather its personality has already developed the psychoses and sheer potential for evil that will make it a menace to society.

The engine is a Chevrolet 406 small block. This is basically a 350 cubic inch V8, but bored out to the max. The heads are aluminium competition items, the carb is bucket sized, and the whole thing is so far back in the chassis that it really needs another little bonnet in the scuttle to get to the racing distributor at the back of the engine.

The bonnet on this car is worth a chapter all on its own. Look at it closely, and you will see it's aluminium. Magnum did make a GRP louvred bonnet which they thought looked not bad at all, given the material it was made from, but the owner of the car said "Close, but no banana. Let's get one hand-formed in aluminium." They made a steel frame, and had an Aston Martin body man make the outer skin. There are loads of louvres all over it, and the scoop is made in such a way that

it's clearly metal and not boring old GRP.

The other clue to the seriousness of this customer and his car is in the wheels. They are American custom five-spokes, of a type very popular in the late Sixties and early Seventies, frequently seen on Chevrolet Camaros. On which they looked the absolute business. To get the wide offset wheels under the arches meant shortening the rear wishbones and driveshafts, and a whole new stress analysis job on the modified rear end. With the best will in the world, this can't have been cheap, but the wheels themselves were sensibly priced. As a bonus, they bolt straight on to Jag hubs. When you look at those wheels shod in fat Pirellis, and compare them to the usual expensive and very familiar Halibrand replicas, there's no contest.

Can I take it for a brief spin? Yes, but watch it, because it's an evil bastard of a thing. The owner is a

Below: Suspension both front and back is pretty serious. There are no half measures here.
Bottom: Engine is a Chevy 350ci bored out to 406ci while gearbox is a modified T10 with remote shift sourced from a Nascar racer.

Wheels came from the States and look the business. Out on the road this Magnum is one mean mother. No mercy for those that don't tell it who is boss. Just how I like it!

bit smaller than me, and the pedals are at an odd angle - but this is adjusted to exactly the way he likes it, so fair enough. The gearbox is a modified T10, with a remote shift sourced from a Nascar racer: it's a pig to use compared to the T10 I was using the previous week in the Dax, which was a real pussycat. This one needs two hands to clank it into reverse.

Ignition on, and a furious buzzing from behind tells me there are some stonking fuel pumps wanging buckets of four-star into the carb, and I have to punch the start button quick or they'll flood the engine. The starter grunts with effort, and finally overcomes the compression to kick the engine over. Nothing happens. A big poke on the throttle, and the engine blasts into life and then as quickly dies. Once more, and the car rocks as the engine explodes into life and dies again.

This thing simply won't tick over. What the hell size is the cam, I ask, and Mike just grins at me. The camshaft must have lobes the size of Pamela Anderson's implants, and something like the same shape. Right, pumps on, push the button and stomp the throttle, blat blat roar, keep it going on the throttle and let it warm up. No choke is needed when you can squirt a pint of juice down the barrels with the accelerator jets. Get it going as smoothly as it ever will, slip the clutch in first, and drive off down the farm road out to the Fosse Way, a Roman road with not many bends. It's been resurfaced since Caesar's day, however, and the legionnaires in chariots have all been replaced by reps in Cavaliers.

It's half a mile or so to the road, and the engine is warming up nicely. Stop, look right and left, hold Mummy's hand and let the clutch in. Bollocks, stalled it. This engine won't even run under about 3000. Poke blam rumble. Give it some juice, dump the clutch, get rolling, then snatch second and open her up a bit. A huge lump of power rockets the whole car forward like a go kart going over a land mine. Clunk click third, woof and we're off again. This is supposed to be a 450 BHP engine, although it feels more like 550. You're right down on the deck and the suspension feels absolutely sorted. No banging about, but no unnecessary movement at all.

Any delicacy in gearchanging leaves you floundering in neutral, so you just have to tell it who's boss. Double declutch, pull it sharply into second, a good bootful and we're away again, third, fourth. As it's a customer's car I'm only allowed a brief spin, so I have to head back for the farm just as I'm beginning to get the hang of the car. Blat from the sidepipes, double declutch, clonk into third, same for second, back into the entrance and over the speed bumps very slowly. Ground clearance is 4" and the speed bumps are 3.75" high. Feather the clutch and keep the engine going, as it wants to stall at anything under 20 MPH. This car is an absolute bitch, and I think I may have fallen in love.

Magnum are now located in the outbuildings that used to house the toys of the late and lamented designer William Towns, who was responsible for some beautiful and radical designs: it's rather nice to feel that there is still automotive innovation going on in the same place.

Magnum are now in the same sort of position as Cobretti in the market place, and for the same reasons. A big factory and overheads are fine while there are lots of orders, but when economic depression stops the orders, the overheads stay the same. The crunch came for Magnum in 1992, but it was mostly the landlord and the tax man who lost out: one customer's car was unfinished, but Mike took that one home and finished it himself. Nowadays, the overheads are reasonable, the landlady is delightful, and Magnum do engine work and fabrication work as well as Magnum kits: they only need to sell the occasional high-spec car to stay comfortably in the black.

A basic Magnum chassis and body kit retails for under four grand, and you could expect to finish a car to a reasonable standard for about £15,000. Not bad at all when you think about the cost of rose joints and Kevlar.

Chapter 20
BACK TO BASICS

The BRA 289 is enjoying a fresh lease

of life with new owners

Tyler Industrial Mouldings:

the improvements are subtle

but significant.

THE BRA WAS BASICALLY NOT A BAD CAR AT ALL, and it was always possible to build something excellent out of the kit. However, the build manual was less than comprehensive, and some builders were driven to biting off their own legs in rage and frustration unless they learned to take a laid-back approach to fitting everything together.

However, John Berry and Peter Ibbotson

Below: Classic 289 lines hold an appeal all of their own. BRA name is now seeing a new lease of life under Tyler Industrial Mouldings.

Top: Rear lights are historically correct, but will set you back up to £140 if you can find some! Above: Interior detailing on this privately built car is no slave to replication. Beautifully tidy, though.

conceived the project and let it potter along for the first fourteen or so years of its life because they wanted to do it that way, so fair enough. They were classic car enthusiasts rather than an ambitious kit car company, and the market for the early 289 shape was, and always will be, relatively limited.

The name Tyler Industrial Mouldings may ring a bell amongst yachties, as the company build a lot of boats. They also build replica bodies for Daimler Darts, which many people may not even have heard of. Making the Dart was a very weird thing for the Daimler company to do, as it was a radical and stylistically outrageous fibreglass two-seater sports car with a small V8: not exactly the sort of thing you would associate with the Daimler image. It's as if the Royal Philharmonic suddenly released a hip hop version of Carmen performed in the nude: there has never been a Daimler like it before or since.

Tyler also build bodies for the Reliant Scimitar, a car which leaves a sour taste in my mouth. I was recently given one, which I'd been looking forward to: unfortunately a Scimitar with a rotten chassis is scrap, just like any production car with a rotten monocoque. The point behind all this sidetracking is that Tyler are well set up for making kit cars, as they already have a profitable GRP car body business.

In the BRA, they saw a very pretty car that only needed minor fiddling to be a very good product indeed: they could extend their car activities at little cost, rather than having to set up a whole new business.

The BRA is more or less an MGB V8, rebodied. Of course, it's lighter, faster, handles better, looks immeasurably better and won't have to be reshelled every five years if you leave it out in the rain. Actually, it's not like an MGB at all, is it? However, it is made from MGB bits. The MG provides the front crossmember and most of the steering, suspension and brakes, the rear axle complete with springs, the handbrake, the door hinges and locks, the pedal box, and a whole pile of bits and pieces that total up to quite a lot of dosh if you have to buy them separately rather than stripping them out of a single donor.

Next, you need a Rover V8. You can still buy one new with a five-speed gearbox from Rover, and you might as well buy a 3.9 litre one while you're at it. Or you can buy an SD1 Rover V8 with a short MOT and no smoke or funny noises coming from the engine, and save loads of money. Either way, you don't actually need to scrap an MGBGTV8, which would cost lots of money and would upset lots of slow sports car enthusiasts. Of course, you could scrap a damaged or rusty four-cylinder MGB and use its engine and gearbox as well, which would provide you with a reliable 1800cc long-stroke Austin Cambridge engine that will bumble along cheaply and reliably, and that will make some quite nice noises too.

The reason that the BRA looks the business is that it was actually moulded from a real 289 Cobra, rather than ten generations down from a 427. The sides of the car taper in as the body drops to the sills, and there is a delicacy of line that is missing from most of the more muscly versions of the car. Another clue to the aluminium origins of the body is the thickness of the rolltop around the edge of the dash and doors. On most replicas, this has developed to a natural thickness for GRP, whereas on the BRA it still looks like a rolled or wired metal body panel.

The passenger door looks slightly concave, and one builder several years ago sent one back to be checked: yes, it was exactly right. That was the shape of the door on John Atkins' original 289, so that's the shape of the door on the BRA. After all, these were hand-made cars, and exactly the same applies even to more mass produced cars like the Jaguar XK120: those are not all the same shape, as I have personally found out to my cost in trying to replicate them.

I've also watched someone rebuilding a badly

Below: Engine bay will damage your eyes on a sunny day! Everything that could be polished or chromed has been. 3.9-litre Rover V8 is a dream, with loads of lazy torque and effortless power.

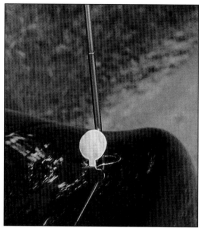

Above right: Typical neat touch on this customer built car is the fantastic aerial cover. Above: Not totally faithful to the original, this interior's still quite tasty.

crashed 260, the forerunner of the 289. Given the method of construction, it's amazing that they came out even vaguely symmetrical. The two main chassis drainpipes are easy enough to align, but the superstructure is a tracery of thin tubes supporting a mostly single skin aluminium shell. You could pretty well pick up the whole body assembly on your own and walk around with it. Which is why they went like a woopsy off a shiny shovel when Shelby started cramming huge engines into them, which in turn is why we're still making replicas of them.

The chassis under the BRA is a very simple and old-fashioned affair, quite in keeping with the rest of the car. It's a straightforward ladder frame, in hefty section steel with various crossmembers to beef it up. It wouldn't look out of place in any classic car restoration workshop, except of course that it's a lot thicker than any production car chassis would ever be: but then it is a kit car, and there are no accountants telling the designers to save a few pence by making the chassis out of tinfoil.

The original wooden back panel and floor panels are now being replaced by composite GRP, and there is talk of Kevlar reinforcement as well. Most of the new changes to the car are of this type, just small detailed improvements. The bonnet skin, for example, is now double skinned. That of course creates its own problems, as the new bonnet is too heavy to be hinged from the GRP bodywork, and has to be hung from a new framework under the front. Not to worry, because the radiator frame is mildly revised as well. The old engineering adage about one change resulting in ten more changes you hadn't thought of is well underlined here. The steering column route is due for a rethink, and a shorter remote gearchange is already on offer.

The Tyler people are cheerfully beavering away getting the car the way they want it. The demonstrator they're building now is also a semi-prototype, with lots of fettling going on, so it's quite a long process. The car will finish up more or less still a BRA, but easier to build, and the plan ultimately is to go for type approval and to build finished cars. This is frequently a good thing, as time-consuming and difficult build problems are generally designed out pretty sharpish by people who have to earn a living building the cars themselves.

On the other hand, those who develop grandiose ideas about getting up above the kit car market and only making finished cars for lots of dosh frequently come to a sticky end. Tyler seem to have their feet on the ground, however, and I have a feeling they'll quite like getting involved with the fellow enthusiasts who are their future customers: that's all part of the fun for most kit car companies.

As the emergent Tyler BRA demonstrator/ prototype was unfinished at the time of writing, owner John Hill brought his own BRA-supplied car over for a photo session. This one is very recently finished, and John is busy writing a proper manual to replace the few photocopied sheets that had previously constituted the manual. The new manual even has an index, which is a bit flash.

John's car is decidedly tasty, with a brand new 3.9 litre Rover V8 and a five-speed box. The rest of the mechanicals are revamped MGB. The car is not really much different to future BRAs, apart from a thinner bonnet and a few details. The colour is as accurate as possible to an AC dark blue originally provided by Pinchin Johnson. One of John's two cats jumped on to the bonnet when the last-but-one coat was still not quite dry. The cat is still alive, but it was wandering around in a fetching shade of blue for some time after it got within range.

The rear lights are the historically correct items, fitted to AC Cobras and to Hillman Californians, but their price has suffered somewhat from inflation since people realised they fitted quarter million pound cars as well as pudgy little Hillmans. When you wanted a new light for a Hillman in the fifties it would cost you 12/6d. Nowadays, they change hands at £140.

The engine bay is pretty dazzling if you open the bonnet in bright sunlight. Everything that could be chromed or polished has been, and if it couldn't be chromed or polished it was braided in shiny metal braid. If it was ally, it was engine turned. That's actually a fairly simple process, involving a rotating abrasive disc on the end of a drill: however, to get it looking anything much at all it takes more patience and dexterity than I like to think about: John probably spent more time on his engine turning than I spent working for my degree. Mind you, I had lots of interruptions to deal with, like drinking, debauchery and mountain climbing.

John's interior is pretty damn tasty too, with door pockets and cable operated door catches, and ashtrays let into the doors. This does strike me as optimistic: ever heard the expression "about as useful as an ashtray on a motorbike"? The cockpit of a moving Cobra, replica or real, is more windy than a vegetarian restaurant with a good reputation for bean salads. Even the rather ambitious stainless steel and glass sidescreens aren't going to do much about that. Anybody who opens one of the ashtrays when the car is moving will get an earful of dog-ends as they whirlwind out into the slipstream.

The dash is non-original, which has the advantage that you can see the instruments without having a steering wheel specially made. The original wheel was an equally spaced three-spoke, with the top spoke pointing upwards, so you could look through it and see the speedo and rev counter. If you haven't got that sort of wheel, the only practical option is to fit the instruments somewhere you can see them.

The floor in the BRA is quite high, as it's on top of the ladderframe chassis, and this means that the simplest way to secure the seats is just to choose where you want them and bolt them to the floor. Tyler are currently investigating very flat runners, but using thin cushions on the seats can give you a perfectly good seating position. A BRA 427 I once drove had full thickness seats and runners, and it felt as though you were sitting on the car rather than in it. However, this didn't occur to me when I climbed into John's car, so he must have got it sorted out.

The exhausts are effective underfloor

ones, and you know it's a V8, but the noise is subtle and understated. It's possible to get a Rover to sound like a rabid pit bull with a hot poker in one end and a microphone taped to the other end: I drove a Cobretti once with an overbored Rover, a wild cam, a huge Holley and four-inch sidepipes with no silencers at all, and it made my ears ring. However, the Rover engine can also be persuaded to speak softly and carry a big stick, which is much more the sort of thing for this car.

The engine is still squeaky clean and brand new, with only a few hundred miles on the clock, so there was no chance of any valve-bouncing and tyre-ripping games. However, even taking it relatively easy, the BRA is capable of quite respectable performance across country. I was particularly impressed that it felt completely solid on the road at an indicated 100 mph.

The suspension is not going to compare with an independent rose jointed multi-adjustable set-up, but then neither is the price. At the front you get double wishbones and a coilover shocks, and at the back you get a live axle and cart springs, similarly taken from the MG. However, an anti-tramp bar and a Panhard rod with adjustable shocks will go a long way to getting the back end to behave itself, and the MGB always handled fairly adequately anyway: the trouble was that it never went fast enough for most people to find that out.

If you fancy one of these, as lots of us will, you can either build it yourself or have a word with Sheridan Bowie at Tyler's: they're quite happy to do partial or complete builds, and if they come out anything like John Hill's car, there will be no complaints.

Below: Classic 289 lines are ultimately more British than the brawny 427.

Appendix
WHERE TO FIND THEM

AK SPORTSCARS
2 Orchard Lane, Woodnewton, Peterborough PE8 5EE. Telephone 01780 470588/01664 454651.

AUTOBRASS
Silverdale, Barfield Close, Dolton, Winkleigh, Devon.

BRA
The Shipyard, Vicarage Lane, Hoo, Rochester, Kent ME3 9LB. Telephone 01634 252709.

BROOKER
Unit 8, Tinkers Drove, Wisbech, Cambridgeshire. Telephone 01945 587778.

CLASSIC REPLICAS
137 Lowther Road, Bournemouth BH8 8NP. Telephone: 01202 241025.

COBRA REPLICA CLUB
Carolyn Hobbes, 01403 255525.

COBRETTI
22 Hillfield Ave, Morden, Surrey SM4 6BA. Telephone 0181 395 0109.

CONTEMPORARY
Waring House, Waring Street, West Norwood SE27 9LH. Telephone: 0181 7666987.

CRENDON REPLICAS
Unit 52, Westcott Venture Park, Westcott, Nr Aylesbury, Bucks HP18 0XB. Telephone 01296 651985, 01844 237370.

DJ SPORTSCARS
2 Edinburgh Place, Harlow, Essex CM20 2DJ. Telephone 01279 442661.

GARDNER DOUGLAS
Pinfold Lane, Bottesford, Nottingham NG13 0AR. Telephone 01949 843299.

MAGNUM
The Barn, Park Farm, Compton Verney, Warwickshire CV35 9HJ. Telephone 01926 642122.

PILGRIM CARS
Unit 14, Mackley Industrial Estate, Small Dole, Henfield, Sussex BN5 9XJ. Telephone 01273 493860.

RAM AUTOMOTIVE
Ram House, Beckingham Business Park, Tolleshunt Major, Malden, Essex CM9 8LZ. Telephone 01621 869123.

ROADCRAFT
Unit 15, Winston Business Centre, Chartwell Road, Churchill Industrial Estate, Lancing, West Sussex BN15 8TU. Telephone 01903 851900.

About the Author

Born in 1954, Iain Ayre was perhaps just old enough to witness the AC Cobra's dramatic climb straight into the automotive history books. Then again, he was probably playing with his first Meccano set! Never one to tread the path of normality, Iain has seen his working career quickly change from a worryingly ordinary spell in teaching, through photography and the world of advertising before finally ending up writing for all manner of rather more fitting alternative motoring titles. His scribblings can often be witnessed in such great tomes as *Fast Ford, Classic Cars, Which Kit?, Ford Heritage* and *Motor Caravan World* (!). Playing with Maseratis, Ferraris and TVRs have all ended up with books being published, *Cobra Replicas* being the most recent.